The Way I Remember It

The Way I Remember It

By
Susan D. Smith

E-BookTime, LLC
Montgomery, Alabama

The Way I Remember It

Library of Congress Control Number: 2009902704

ISBN: 978-1-60862-011-1

First Edition
Published March 2009
E-BookTime, LLC
6598 Pumpkin Road
Montgomery, AL 36108
www.e-booktime.com

Dedication

I dedicate this book to all my family and friends, most of all to my husband, Mike. He encouraged me to do this and gave me the means to do it. Thank you, Mike!

"People who live in glass houses shouldn't throw stones."
    ——*Geoffery Chaucer's "Troilus and Criseyde" (1385)*

"I can't throw stones at glass houses because mine has shattered so many times, sometimes I wonder if there is even a foundation left."
    ——*Susan Smith on her roller coaster life (2007)*

"I am who I am because of events and people who have touched my life."   ——*Susan Smith (2005)*

Contents

Contents

Introduction

I am not what you would call a famous person. I am sure some people will look at my name and figure I am writing this book from my prison cell, but I am not *that* Susan Smith. So why am I writing a book? - Because I love to laugh and tell stories. It is a good thing I love to laugh, because there is plenty to laugh about in my life and do I ever have stories!

The first time I ever showed any interest in writing was when I was in senior high school. A teacher wanted us to write current events every day. A friend of mine and I were bored doing the same thing every day. Instead of going to the library like we were supposed to do, we waited for the teacher to leave and we went back to the empty classroom. We made up a story. It had to do with a man who had an accident and lost his arm and he never did find it. This went on with a few more body parts. I handed it in to the teacher and regretted it almost immediately. I was sure I was in *sooooo* much trouble. He read it and laughed! He said "this is really good but it is not a current event." I guess he knew IT WAS A BIG FAT LIE! However, he suggested putting it in the school newspaper, (which I never did) and also to do a real current event if I wanted a passing grade.

My family, who is my inspiration, gives me an awful lot of good material to write about as you will soon find out as you read the book. My friends manage to contribute material for me as well, though unwittingly.

Through all the trials and tribulations in my life, someone always gives me something to laugh about. With these people in my life, I can survive anything. Each story is my memory, the way I remember it.

Country Living

I grew up in Brookston, Minnesota. Actually, I grew up in Culver, north of Brookston but no one knows where that is and our mail came out of Brookston in the later years. I just *know* everyone knows where Brookston is! Oh all right, you can barely see it on the map, but if you check out where Duluth is, Brookston is just 32 miles west of Duluth. The population is just under 100 people or at least it was a few years ago. *It fluctuates, due to the fact that there are deaths and births.*

As you take Highway 31 north, you will cross the Stony Brook. Hopefully, if you visit the bridge will still be there. It is in rough shape, but if you don't look under it you'll never know. I prefer not to meet anyone on it, because if the bridge goes, I would rather go down by myself. At least then I have a better chance of surviving the crash. The brook isn't all that deep; most of the time, so chances are a person isn't going to drown anyway. The Stony Brook is on the south side of Brookston.

The town is situated in the middle of Culver Township on the Fond du Lac Indian Reservation. The St. Louis River runs along the north side of town with railroad tracks next to it. The bridge used to be a Truss bridge but in the last twenty years or so it has been modernized. The river divides Brookston and Culver, as well as the Fond du Lac Indian Reservation. The Artichoke River flows into the St. Louis on the north side of town.

My husband Mike and I are fortunate to live on the hill overlooking the two rivers. It is like a piece of heaven on earth. We are surrounded by a variety of trees: pine, cedar, birch, oak and elm that give us the desired privacy. On our back deck we are able to look down the hill at the Artichoke River. We have meandering trails through the woods we mow in summer and we often take walks there. It is my favorite spot to visit, to relieve stress and to find a sense of peace. The ferns that border the trails, stand about five feet tall, during the summers we have rain. In dry summers they're dead.

The Artichoke is a winding river with trees on both sides and an old fashioned bridge over it. There are huge rocks in the river that we can sit on when the river is low. I guess we could sit on them when it is high too, but I much prefer breathing in the fresh air, rather than water. A gravel road divides our property on the south side. Across this road is the St. Louis River where we are able to fish. At night we can look out our living room window and see all the lights in town. It is a pretty site, all four houses. That might be a slight exaggeration; there are a *few* more houses than that.

People may say Brookston is a dying town, but to those of us who live here we know better. We still have everything we *really need* like the local bar and a church. We have a post office; you just can't work a day job and expect to be able to go into the post office. It is only open when you are at work. *It must make for some long days for the postmaster.* Luckily, a lot of people have their mail delivered. You may not always get your own mail but it helps to know everyone in town. You can always exchange mail, even though you are not supposed to do that, so I have been told.

The local Lutheran Church is a quaint little church situated on a hill as you drive into town. Behind this church is where the Brookston School was. It was a high school when my dad attended, but an elementary school when I attended. It has since been torn down and the children go to a school in Saginaw. Not in Michigan, that would be one *helluva* commute. Across from this church is a Catholic Church that has been renovated into a community center that the Fond du Lac Indian Reservation owns. It is called "The Lavonne (Dottie) Smith Center" after my mother-in-law. It now stands empty.

As you drive down the hill there are a couple of unpaved streets. One of them even has a stop sign that most people ignore. *Not me of course.* To the left you will find the U.S. Post Office. Across from there, there is another unpaved street that leads to the ballpark and town hall. After passing the post office there are a couple of other buildings, one that is brick and used to be a bank, *waaaay before my time*. There is a road to the left and believe it or not, that one IS paved and has a stop sign. Most people stop for this one, however; I cannot vouch for the ones leaving the local business. This road leads to the bar and what used to be a grocery store. The grocery store is boarded up, but the bar is still there. It started out as the Legion, but was sold many years ago to private owners.

The people of Immanuel Lutheran Church are very laid back. On a good day, there may be sixty parishioners. My family always sat in the third row from the front of the church. You ask me why? I don't know. We took up the whole pew too. There was my father, mother, me and my four sisters. To this day, we can come into the church and think, *"There sure aren't many people in church today."* By the time the pastor starts the sermon; we can look around and see the church has filled up! We have no concept of time apparently. In my family we call being late as being on "Hansen Time." You will learn more about "Hansen Time" later.

There used to be a Co-op and feed store, but that closed many years ago. Other businesses have come and gone. We much prefer patronizing bigger stores, in bigger towns, rather than our local ones. We sure would hate to see anyone make a go of it here. Truthfully, there are people who make a point of patronizing the local establishments. Stony Brook Saloon seems to have business. They must sell what some residents are looking for. Go figure!

A lot of people commute to nearby cities to work. When I say cities I mean mostly Duluth or Cloquet. City people would say it takes approximately twenty minutes to get to Cloquet and about thirty minutes to Duluth, unless my husband Mike is driving, then tack on another ten minutes or so. Cloquet is twenty miles away and Duluth is about thirty-two miles.

The biggest event in Brookston is the 4th of July. *It is held on July 4th of every year.* It started out many, many years ago with races for the kids. The Legion and Auxiliary were in charge of everything. My dad would gather up gunny sacks, rope for the three legged race and eggs for the egg toss. He would call "ON YOUR MARK, GET SET, and GO!" All the children in that age group would take off. The first place winner would get fifty cents, the second place winner would receive twenty-five cents, third place a dime and everyone else would get a nickel. Everyone was a winner. After the races we could run to the candy store and buy *a lot* of candy. Those were the good old days, let me tell you. We were able to buy big amounts of candy with that change and still stay thin after eating it all. Of course, nowadays, some of us are not seen running races before we go buy that little bit of candy with our dollar bills.

My mother and my aunt would sell pop out of big round tubs filled with ice. They had to open the cans with can openers; there were no tabs on the cans then. Every now and then one would explode and they would be covered in pop - that is what we Minnesotans call soda. They always wore big straw hats to prevent sunburn. I am not so sure the hats worked because by the end of the afternoon, their faces were the color of ripe tomatoes. I suppose it could have been the strawberry pop that exploded, now that I think about it.

After the races everyone would either head to the bar or go home for their family picnics. My family always opted for the family picnic at my parent's farm. There would be volleyball, badminton and croquet to play; as well as lots of food to eat and mostly non-alcoholic beverages to drink. At nine o'clock everyone would head back down to the ball park for the fireworks. My dad ordered the fireworks and he and other legionnaires would fire them off after dark. After the fireworks, some of the adults would head to the bar again to attend the dance with *live* music, meaning no juke box, a real band. I don't want you to get the idea we used dead people for entertainment when we didn't have live music, we had too much class for that.

Eventually, the women in the Legion Auxiliary came up with the idea of having a parade. The first year, people rode bikes, horses or maybe dressed up and walked. The parade went around town twice, *makes it nice if you missed something the first time around.* Of course, you best be on time, because those who were five minutes late, missed the parade. Over the years, it has become bigger and better. It is the only time of year that both sides of the street are full of people. The parade still goes around town twice, but even if you are late you will probably be able to catch it the second time around. As a matter of fact, it has gotten so big now, that people on the floats may actually run out of candy to throw to the spectators the second time around.

Labor Day used to be another big event in Brookston. The Legion sponsored an auction every year at the bar. People could bring in items to have auctioned off and give the club 10% of their profits. My dad did a lot of the auctioneering. He wasn't a professional, but he got the job done. Like many other things, the auction is history.

The Legion sponsored a lot of dances. There were the Hunters' Balls, (Who came up with that name? Not me!) New Year's Eve Dances, Sadie Hawkins' Dances, Halloween Masquerades and anything else they could think of to have a dance for. Let me go back to the Hunters' Balls for a second, I really don't want you to get the wrong idea about us. We weren't celebrating the *Hunters' Balls*. Every year during hunting season there would be a dance just because it was hunting season and they called it the Hunters' Ball. No, it wasn't for some poor hunter who had a hunting accident and now only has one. Trust me; we would not think to celebrate that! Anyway, everyone had a blast at these balls; I mean fun at these dances!

One year there was an April fool's Dance. My mother, known as The Poster Girl, (she wasn't on the poster, she just always made them) and my aunt made the posters to put around town, advertising the big dance. There were some big names. Johnny Cash, Ray Stevens, Loretta Lynn, you know the usual big names that jump at the chance to play in Brookston, Minnesota. When people got to the dance, some were very disappointed to learn they were on the juke box! Those who weren't too upset by the April fool's joke stayed and had a great time. There was a door prize. You guessed it, it was a door.

One of my favorite dances was the Halloween Masquerade. My sister April and I decided to go as hookers. Her husband Randy was our pimp. We had play money that we had to hand over to our pimp. Of course, we dressed the part and had plenty of make-up on our faces. I'm sorry to say, one person told me I looked like Tammy Wynette. Go figure! I guess that would make me one classy hooker then. Randy, was a little nervous about showing up in our costumes, because my parents would be there. They're April's parents too, even though we like to deny it sometimes. He was afraid they might be shocked to see their daughters in these getups. Anyway, when we got there, there were my upstanding parents dressed as Marshal Dillon and Miss Kitty from the television show "Gunsmoke." MY MOTHER WAS THE MADAM! Now who's shocked? Dad really got into the swing of things. He kept confiscating our money and arresting us for prostitution.

Not everything in Brookston was centered on the bar. Well, maybe most of it was before the Legion was sold to private owners. Okay, maybe even after that, but hey the same people who closed down the bar Saturday night, were sitting in their favorite pew in church on Sunday morning. Well, maybe not every Sunday, but most of the time.

There is one other event I just have to mention, because "the big city" people in Duluth, Cloquet or one of the other nearby "big cities" love to poke fun at the small town of Brookston. Every year in the spring the ice breaks up on the St. Louis River. They think it is hilarious that people stand on the bridge watching it float down the river. It is a sure sign of spring when that happens. *The ice breaking up, not the city people making fun, they do that year round.*

19

The Hansen Clan

I grew up on an eighty acre farm. My parents raised beef cattle. Besides me, there were four other girls, Robin, April, Brenda and Gayle. There are fifteen years between the oldest and the youngest. People sometimes made the mistake of thinking Robin or I was Gayle's mother. It was funny then, not so funny now.

The Hansen Clan extended to a family of pets, as well. We had cats, dogs, more cats, a goose, more cats, a lamb and *waaaaaaaay* too many cats. The cats lived in the barn for the most part.

Every morning, before my sisters and I left for school, we took turns feeding those cats. As soon as one of us stepped out the door with their food, there would be several cats already waiting. We would yell, HERE KITTY, KITTY, KITTY as we walked toward the shack where they were fed. As we were walking, there would be about twenty cats following us. The rest of them were already in the shack waiting.

My parents were not only husband and wife, they were best friends. They did almost everything together. Not only did they go to those Saturday night dances and Sunday church services, but they worked on the farm together. Summers were spent haying and sometimes, the haying didn't get completely done before the first snowfall. During haying season, mom would run errands when the machinery broke down and dad needed parts. She spent *a lot* of time doing errands. That also explains why we were haying until the first snow fall.

When dad was working his paying job, Mom would be busy doing household chores and yard work. She would also do extra jobs, like clean out the garage. What a nice thing to do for dad.

I remember one such day when mom decided to clean the garage. Anyone who ever saw the inside of my dad's garage knew what an undertaking that was. Dad believed in saving everything. He was often heard saying "you just never know this might come in handy someday." Mom didn't believe that way. They were close, but they had their separate minds. While she was cleaning the garage, my uncle stopped by and later told my aunt, "that Diane, she was cleaning the garage and she was pitching things out the door left and right, I never saw anyone clean so fast!"

Mom had put in a full day of work on the garage and had a pile of junk ready for Dad to throw into the back of the pick-up and take to the dump. It would probably take at least two or three trips to the dump. I was not living at home anymore and mom called me to tell me about her day of cleaning. She felt good about accomplishing so much. She repeated what my uncle had told auntie about the way she cleaned the garage. She said "Dad is outside, which is where they kept the pick-up and garage, loading up the truck for the dump." She looked out the window and suddenly said, "OH THAT GUY, *YOU WON'T BELIEVE* WHAT HE'S DOING. HE'S PUTTING MOST OF THAT JUNK BACK INTO THE GARAGE!" Wanna bet? I was glad she couldn't see me because I had a vision of Dad pitching everything back into the garage left and right and needless to say, I was laughing and she wasn't. IT WAS MOM IN REVERSE! The funny thing was, dad never did anything fast but I think the adrenaline kicked in when it came to saving his junk.

As I mentioned, my dad did everything slow. He even talked slow. He did not waste words. Every word that came out of his mouth was carefully thought out, before he said it. Mom would patiently wait for him to finish talking, even through the long pauses. There were times when my sisters and I would come running into the house to tell mom about something and she would say "hush, dad is talking." We would stop talking and impatiently wait. Even though it was quiet when we walked in, we knew dad well enough to know, he was talking. It was just a matter of time before we would hear evidence of that.

On the few occasions when mom and dad did things separately, like going to the women's Bible Study, dad would miss her. I remember going to their house and dad was working in the yard. We talked and he offered me coffee, which surprised me, because in all the years I was growing up, dad never so much as opened the refrigerator door and he absolutely did not cook or make coffee. We went into the house and wonders never cease, he offered me lunch and proceeded to get the sandwich makings out. We had a great lunch and conversation. I had plenty of time to chew my food while dad was talking.

Hansen Time

For as long as I can remember, my dad was never on time to anything, except work. He drove cement truck for many years until he developed asthma and could not be around the dust anymore. He became a school bus driver and people would often comment, "You can set the clock by Lawrence Hansen." WHO WAS THAT MAN, I ASK? Let me tell you about the man I knew.

Every year my great-aunt would have Thanksgiving dinner. Every year they would hold dinner for our family, because we were late. Remember, I mentioned people coming into church late? My family - some still come in late, hence the "Hansen Time."

In 1977, I graduated from high school. I was late getting to graduation. My dad was getting ready and my mother never tried to rush him. To do that would only make it worse. I remember running to the Home-Economics room to put my cap and gown on. My home-room teacher scolded me for being late. I tried to explain it wasn't my fault but I don't think she understood "Hansen Time."

It wasn't always Dad's fault. As I mentioned before, we lived on a farm and there would be times we were ready to leave for a wedding or some event and the cows would get out. That meant herding them back into the fence that always seemed to need fixing. Of course, the cows believed the "grass is greener on the other side of the fence," and did not always cooperate. Oh well, there was always the reception to go to, or more likely the dance.

My dad was always on "Hansen Time" when it came to remodeling the house too. Dad was a perfectionist when it came to working on the house. To hang a piece of trim he could be seen looking at the spot over and over, measuring and re-measuring. He was in *thinking* mode then. Eventually, he would move on to *doing* mode, maybe even the same day. I once asked my Uncle Gordon if he does that too and he said, "Yeah, you know first you have to think about it and then you think about it some more and once you think about it enough, then you have to decide, if that is what you want to do. Once you decide you want to do it, you have to think about how you want to do it; you can't just jump into it. You have to mull that around in your head for awhile. Eventually, you decide how you want to do it and then you use extreme caution and start doing it. Measuring many times, to make sure you get it right the first time, otherwise you have to go back to the beginning again." Okay, *maybe* I exaggerated that a little, but for the most part, that is what he told me.

My dad inherited this trait from his mother which makes her my grandmother, believe it or not. Grandma loved to bake. She made the best banana bread. Apparently, she thought so too because she treated it as a masterpiece. As a child I could not wait to sink my teeth into a piece of that banana bread. I would stand and watch her slice it *perfectly.* She would slice, stop, look to see if it were even, slice some more, stop and look again. She would do this for every slice. Now that I think about it, it was very similar to how dad did his remodeling jobs.

I would share Grandma's banana bread recipe, but some prefer to keep it in the family and I want to respect that. However; if you are family, Grandma gave my Aunt Marilyn a copy of it and she has shared it with me and some of my sisters already.

I think you probably have a pretty good idea where "Hansen Time" came from. What you don't know is how many have inherited this trait from my dad. Of all my sisters, besides me, only one has not inherited this trait. We are the two oldest in the family, and then it is my sister, April. She and her family rarely make it to church on time. We all know when they get there, because remember, we sit at the front of the church. Brenda is next, she breezes in, whenever, if at all. Gayle is the youngest. She is always late; however she does try to be on time, if I am driving us somewhere. I threatened to leave her when she was much younger, apparently it still works.

My aunt was visiting from Oklahoma and my husband Mike and I decided to take her and my mother out for the day. Gayle and her family wanted to come as well. I told her the time and that we would swing by her house and they could follow us. Mike was driving, we pulled in, blew the horn, no one came out. I decided to be nice, went in and told them we were ready to leave. Her husband had just poured himself a glass of milk. I am guessing he grew up on "Hansen Time" too. I went out to the van and told Mike to start pulling out of the driveway. He and my aunt looked horrified. My mother, on the other hand, knew and just smiled. Mike started pulling out of the driveway, reluctantly. I let him stop for a second at the end of the driveway and looked back. There they all were, rushing out to their car. We were on our way!

I could go on and on about "Hansen Time" but I think you get the picture. Hansen's were never on time and some still aren't!

The Hansen Look

We not only have "Hansen Time," we also have the dreaded "Hansen Look." Anyone who has had the misfortune to be on the receiving end of one of these looks, probably had nightmares afterward. My dad had this look, one look from him and you froze! It was a sharp look and I don't mean he was a snappy dresser; it was a look like the sharp edge of a saber. Most of his daughters have inherited this look, actually; I think we all have. The good news is the look came in handy when we were raising kids, the bad news - they inherited it too.

What Imaginations!

Growing up on a farm in the sixties and seventies really helped to develop mine and my sisters' imaginations. We did not have video games, computers, a V.C.R. and certainly not a D.V.D. player. We did have a black and white television set and later a color set. We had a phonograph to play our records on too. We're not *that* old! Just in case there are some people too young to know what the phonograph and records were - they were big C.D. players that we played our big C.D.s on.

When we weren't haying we could be found in the hay barn swinging from a rope and landing in a pile of hay at the bottom of the loft. We had a flood in our lower pasture one year and decided it made a really cool swimming hole. We jumped in and saw "cow pies" floating by. They were the real McCoy too. This is where our imaginations came in. In our minds, they were just "lily pads."

When my sisters and I were growing up, we had a spot between the yard and the hayfield that we would call "the picnic woods." I am not really sure why we called them that, because we rarely ate there, because of mosquitoes. I guess, maybe the mosquitoes had quite a picnic. We usually only went there when we were in trouble or to avoid going to Sunday school. We thought we were pretty smart because we figured we wouldn't be found. Being a little smarter now, I think our parents knew where we were, but it worked to their benefit, since they had been to one of those Saturday night dances.

Mom had her spanking stick, yes, in those days spankings were allowed and we survived. I remember one time taking the stick off the nail by the refrigerator and throwing it into "the picnic woods." That was real clever, I didn't think about the fact that it was easily replaced and was. At least she didn't find out until now. *I so hope she doesn't still have one of those sticks, "the picnic woods" are too far for me to run to now.*

I will let you know, if I ever figure out why we named them "the picnic woods." I can tell you this much, it usually was no picnic when we were running there. It just occurred to me, THAT WAS OUR PUNISHMENT!

I Hate Green Beans!!!

I have absolutely nothing good to say about green beans. They are an awful shade of green, they smell funny and they taste even worse. As a child, they literally made me sick to my stomach and they still do. I grew up in an era where you cleaned your plate or at the very least, ate a little of everything on your plate. Mom liked making those green beans. I would ask mom, if I could eat in the bedroom. Once in awhile, she would okay this. I always made sure I only asked on the nights we had green beans. I can be very inventive when the need arises. I said inventive, not smart. I knew mom didn't clean behind the dresser everyday, so it was the perfect hiding place. I reached over the dresser and scraped my plate. I didn't always stop at just the green beans either. This went on for weeks, maybe even months, I cannot remember that part. What I do remember is coming home from school one day and one look on mom's face and I knew I was busted! People say when you have been married a long time you begin to look like your spouse. IT'S TRUE! That "Hansen Look" was on my mother's face. She took one look at me and said, "I HAVE BEEN CLEANING BEHIND THAT DRESSER ALL DAY! IT SMELLED TO HIGH HEAVEN IN THAT BEDROOM AND I HAD TO SCRAPE WALLS, THE DRESSER AND THE FLOOR! WHAT THE HELL IS THE MATTER WITH YOU!!!!!" Actually, I cannot remember everything she said but that is what that "Hansen Look" on her face said.

Family Pranks

Growing up with sisters was never dull. One of my first memories is spending quality time with my baby sister April. Mom and Dad were putting up snow fence in the yard, Robin was attending Head Start, April was sleeping in her crib, and I was; well let's just say, at loose ends. My mother wore bright red lipstick and had many tubes of it in her dresser drawer. I admired it when she would put it on. I figured she didn't need that many and wouldn't miss one. I took it into April's crib to share with her. I helped her put it on. First I took her clothes off and proceeded to color her with it. After I ran out of lipstick and there was still bare skin to cover, I helped myself to another tube. This went on until Robin came home and saw April. She thought the baby was covered in blood. I don't remember much else. Just the horrified looks on my parents' faces and I knew I was in big trouble. I was too young for the "picnic woods" at that point. My bottom matched April, without benefit of the lipstick.

My oldest sister Robin and I loved tormenting April and Brenda. We called them "the little guys." I am pretty sure it was because we thought it put us a cut above them. Who knows? Maybe it did. One of the pranks we played on "the little guys" happened while we were babysitting. Mom and Dad had gone to the Metrodome in the cities for a Twins Game. We Minnesotans call St. Paul and Minneapolis "the cities." We each had our own box of Chiclets Gum. I am sure it was Robin who came up with the idea, being as clever as she was or just plain mean, it couldn't have been me, of course, especially since this is the way I choose to remember it. If you ever heard of Feenamint Gum, you probably can guess what comes next. We replaced our gum in the box with the Feenamint, which is a laxative. We offered to share our gum with "the little guys." It never occurred to them to wonder why we were being so generous. We let them have as much as they wanted. They were greedy little buggers. They spent the rest of the day in the bathroom. I don't know how they did it, since we only had one bathroom; in all likelihood they shared the toilet. It made our job easier as far as babysitting went. Knew where they were at all times. There was hell to pay when mom and dad got home!

Robin and I did not limit our pranks to just our sisters. Dad was a good target, though scary one. Dad had the car parked in the driveway right outside of the kitchen window. We thought it would be really cool to drive it. Robin was about eight, I think and I was seven. Dad knew better than to leave keys in the car with kids around, but who needs keys? Robin knew all about putting the car in neutral. I told you she was clever, all she needed was some muscle. That is where I came in. I pushed, she drove. As we drove by the window, we smiled and waved at dad and our faces fell. Dad was looking out at us and there was no mistaking what he was saying "S.O.B." He didn't abbreviate. Robin flew out of the car and I was on her heels running for "the picnic woods."

On April fool's Day, we all decided to fool Dad. We were all in on this one, I believe. We were standing in the living room in front of the big picture window. We were having trouble with skunks at the time and thought we could be convincing, if we told dad there was one out there. We yelled, "THERE'S A SKUNK IN THE YARD!" We sat back and waited for Dad to come into the room so we could yell, "APRIL FOOL!" Just one problem, he didn't come. He ran straight to the gun cabinet, grabbed his gun and headed for the door. We all sat in the living room looking at each other, dumbfounded. I told Robin, "Tell him April Fool." She said, "No you do it." Tried to get the "little guys" to do it, but they weren't having any of it. Robin finally gathered her courage and took care of business and in a tiny little voice said "APRIL FOOL!" I'm surprised he heard her. We all waited with bated breath and Dad took one look at us fools sitting there and laughed. Whew! That was close.

Some pranks were unintentional. People have often commented on how much my sisters and I look alike. Robin has brown hair, April and Gayle both blonde, - more on that later. I am strawberry blonde when it isn't gray and Brenda has auburn hair. Apparently, people haven't noticed those differences.

One day I went to a rummage sale and later in the day Robin went to the same sale. My husband's co-worker was at the sale, the same time as Robin. Mike's co-worker told him, he saw *me* at the rummage sale and that he had talked to me. I told Mike, "I never saw him."

Robin called to tell me she went to the sale and this guy kept "coming on" to her. He would not leave her alone. He kept following her around and talking to her like they were friends. I asked, "You were nice to him weren't you?" Of course she wasn't because he was "*harassing*" her. I told her "he thought you were me!" After that incident my sisters and I agreed, that when someone talks to us like they know us, we'll go along with it because he or she may know one of the sisters. We make great stalker targets! - potential stalkers - keep the "Hansen Look" in mind.

I don't want to leave you with the impression that Robin and I were the only ones who pulled stunts. "The little guys" were no angels. Mostly, they did it to each other since we were more sophisticated at it. That all changed when they got older and they were no longer "the little guys."

Brenda loves to play April fool's jokes on people. I was working for a facility that provides services for people with disabilities. Brenda had clients that attended there, from her adult foster home. She called and told me the pipes at work had burst, so I didn't have to go to work. SHE LIED! However; I got off easy, the bus driver who picked her clients up to bring them to Floodwood, where the facility was located, asked me "do you know what your sister did to me?" I could only imagine. He told me, that when he pulled into the yard, she came running up to him and said "you just ran over my puppy!" He jumped off the bus, feeling horrible and she said "April Fool!" Just makes you want to slap her, doesn't it? Sometimes, my sisters can just be mean.

Speaking of mean, let me tell you about my sister April. She called me from her job and asked, if I would take her to the doctor, because she was having trouble with her neck and couldn't drive. Being the kind sister that I am, I said I'll be right there. I drove about thirty miles to pick her up and I sat in the waiting room with her for a *really long* time.

The doctor told her she had whiplash and put her in a neck brace. I would tell you how that happened, but I wouldn't want to generate any sympathy for her, BECAUSE SHE DOES NOT DESERVE IT! I will tell you this much, it had something to do with donating blood, passing out and hitting her face on a window crank. She's okay now.

April asked if I wanted to stop at Perkins to get something to eat and she would pay. I said "sure, but you don't have to pay for mine." After we looked at the menus, I asked her if she would order mine, but get separate checks. I needed to use the little girl's room. I came back and April was sitting there with a smirk on her face. I asked her "what?" She laughed and said, "I told the waitress to put it on one check and not to let you have it because you would be *very angry*." The waitress pointed at my neck brace and asked "did she do that?" I told her, "Yes she did." When it came time for the waitress to deliver the check, she wouldn't even look at me; she set the check on the corner of the table farthest away from me and tried not to come any closer than she had to. WELL, that's what I get for being nice to my sister. At least, I did get a free meal out of the deal.

My sister Gayle played the biggest prank on mom and dad! Mom was in her forties when suddenly, she discovers, baby number five is on the way! Mom went to her first doctor appointment and the nurse asked her, "Do you want to keep it?" Mom looked at her like she was crazy. It isn't like she can send it back. The reason I tell you this story is because every year on her birthday, Gayle would give mom flowers and thank her for keeping her. I told Gayle one time, "You'll notice the rest of us don't give mom flowers on your birthday." Just kidding! Okay, so I can be mean too. Truthfully, one of the happier times in my childhood was that baby being born. Don't tell Gayle though, I have a reputation to uphold.

I was shopping at Wal-Mart, where my sister April works. Off in the distance I could see her and tried to catch up to her to see if she wanted to go for lunch. She walked too fast and I could not catch her. When I left the store, I decided to leave her a note on the windshield of her van. I wrote - I saw you, but I couldn't catch you, you were walking too fast. I reread the note and thought to myself, *it sounds like a stalker wrote this.* I did not want anyone to happen by and think I was a stalker, so I signed Brenda's name. I thought it would be funny to confuse both sisters. It worked like a charm.

April left a message for Brenda saying, "I wasn't ignoring you; I was just doing my Wal-Mart walk." Apparently, April's family teased her that the only time she walked fast was when she was at work; they called it her

Wal-Mart walk. Brenda got the message and was baffled by it. She left a message on April's answering machine saying "I have no idea what you are talking about."

In the meantime I confessed to April about what I had done. She left another message for Brenda, "Call Susan, she can explain it." Now Brenda was really confused, *not that it takes much to accomplish this*, but Brenda phoned me and told me, "I got the strangest message from April, she said I saw her and that she was doing her Wal-Mart walk. I have no idea, what that is. She told me to call you, to explain what is going on." I tried not to laugh, but finally had to "fess up." I said, "You must have thought April had really lost her mind". She responded "I already knew that, but I thought she must be getting worse." We really are kind to each other.

My mother's youngest brother, Dickie and I had a special bond. We were NOT nice to each other, but it was all in fun. He was visiting and we were hurling the usual insults at each other. We were celebrating a birthday and there was a Dairy Queen cake. All of a sudden, my uncle picked up the cake box and held it in front of me, the camera was ready. There was my face in the window of the box and outside that window it read, DAIRY QUEEN! I am pretty sure that was meant to be an insult.

For the 4th of July picnic, that we had on July 4th, my sister made bars that I really liked. My Uncle Dickie also liked them, along with a lot of other people. When I went to get one, I was disappointed there weren't any left. My uncle told me he had a secret stash and he was willing to share with me. I could not believe how nice he was being to me. *I was so naïve.* As I was eating the bar, my sister asked, "Where did you find those bars?" I told her about Dickie's secret stash. She laughed and said, "He wouldn't let me throw away the ones I dropped on the ground." I had visions, of all the farm animals running around doing their business and thought, *"you would think I would learn that, if Dickie is being that nice to me, there has to be a reason."* He was laughing his head off!

Sometimes people get the impression that we are mean to each other, I have no clue, why.

Brothers We Never Really Had

Before Gayle was born, a family moved into the area, that my parents became close friends with. There were four girls in our family and they had four boys - Steven, Darren, Daniel and Scott. We spent a lot of time together; we played and fought like any siblings will do. We never thought of each other as anything but brothers and sisters. There may have been crushes here and there but we never acted upon them. However, my dad may have felt differently. He was a little protective of his girls.

One night, the boys were staying over at our house. We had a hunting shack on the property. Steven, Darren, Robin and I thought it would be cool to stay in the shack. There was only one bed, so we all slept on it. When dad walked in he was upset to see us lying on the bed: boy, girl, boy, girl. We were all in trouble that day. I don't think he believed us, when we said it was innocent. Robin and I didn't want to be next to each other and neither did the boys. That was the only solution. After all, it would be bad to get those sibling cooties.

I hate to say this, but we did it again and this time "the little guys" were there too. Meaning our little guys and there little guys, all in a row. I know, that just doesn't sound right, anyway once again it was innocent. However; we do like to tell our husbands, they were the first guys we ever slept with. See, we aren't even nice to our husbands!

The boys helped with the haying in summer, because it was difficult to hay in winter. One year we had a little trouble with our hay wagon. *Like that* was an unusual occurrence. One of the wheels fell off while dad was driving the hay load home from the field. Robin and I were on the wagon along with Steven and Darren. Suddenly, dad turned around when he felt the wagon slant and all he saw, were a bunch of hay bales tumbling down along with arms and legs sticking out. The arms did not belong to those square hay bales so the only other option was; they belonged to the bodies of the kids! He jumped off the tractor and no one ever saw hay bales fly the way they did that day. Robin and Darren had fallen between the wagon and the tractor. Dad was terrified that they had been hurt. Luckily, they weren't, for the most part they came up laughing. Steven and I, we just ended up in the middle of the road with a few bales on top of us - no big deal.

Eventually, the family moved away and we saw very little of them. Many years went by and we heard that their father died. My father had died five years prior. Some of my sisters and I decided to take mom to the funeral in Cook, Minnesota. The oldest boy had to leave before we got there, but we saw the rest of them. We met some of their wives and girlfriends. Let me clarify that, each one either had a wife or a girlfriend, not one of each. We were amazed to learn that people knew of us as "the Hansen girls from Brookston." They never forgot us anymore than we forgot them. They were excited to hear that my husband Mike and I had moved back to Brookston and bought the house they used to live in. We hope to have a reunion at the house and reminisce some more.

When Susan Met Mike

Mike and I knew each other, before we ever started dating. At least, we knew who each other was. We both grew up in Brookston and we both attended the same schools.

When I was a freshman in high school and Mike was a senior, he was running for Homecoming King. I asked my cousin Eva, who she was voting for and she told me Mike and "Jessie." I said I was too, but only because I felt sorry for her because she had run before and not won and she didn't have much of a chance with Mike Smith as her partner. I didn't like him because I thought he was stuck up. I later realized he was shy and you couldn't meet a nicer person. It was many years later that we actually met.

He was home on leave from the army and I was working at the Co-op in Brookston. He came into the store and according to him, he tried to talk to me but I was too stuck up to talk to him. I absolutely, do not recall this, but hey I was working - must have been during a rush, probably we had four or five people in the store at the time.

A couple of years later, we met at the Legion in Brookston. It's amazing how much more courage you have at those Saturday night dances. We struck up a conversation and agreed to meet the next weekend at his brother's wedding dance. I grew up with the bride so I already planned to attend. From that time on, we were together.

We would take long drives along the country roads and stop at a gas station and Mike would buy each of us a can of

Coke and a bag of M & Ms. Mike was unemployed at the time.

Mike and I would spend a lot of time walking in the woods, just enjoying nature. Mike would carry his rifle in case he saw any partridge or grouse as he would call them. He decided I should learn how to shoot, as well. I was reluctant, but he talked me into it, he said "It hardly kicks at all." Being the trusting person that I was, I figured it wouldn't hurt to try. "It knocked me on my ass!" I was fighting mad at this point and told him, "you just wait, I always get revenge!" For those of you who aren't as ignorant about guns as I was, it was a 12 gauge single shot and it DOES KICK!

My opportunity for revenge soon came, on a nice crisp autumn day; we walked up the railroad tracks near my parent's house. Along the way we spotted a beaver dam. They had been busy little beavers. The dam was about the size of a big pond. Mike walked a little closer and bent down. His butt was just too tempting for me as I had flash backs to the day of the gun. My foot connected with his butt and he came up sputtering. Now, *he* was fighting mad! He complained all the way back about how he was probably going to end up with pneumonia. Such drama! To be fair, it was too cold to go swimming that day, but what can I say, I was so traumatized by the rifle incident that all reason flew out of my head. I know more drama!

Eventually, I introduced Mike to family members. When I introduced him to my cousin, I told him "this is Mike Smith." My cousin's response was "yeah right, and I bet you have a brother named John." I had to tell him, "Yeah, he does." That is the absolute truth!

I introduced Mike to my grandmother. We happened to drive through the town she lived in and I suggested we stop in and visit. Mike complimented her on an antique picture she had and she said "after the two of you get married, you can have it." I thought I would die on the spot! We hadn't dated long at that point. Of course we have that picture and it is my insurance that he will not consider divorce, because I would have custody of the picture.

Mike was always such a romantic! He always came up with really cool places to park and make out or "neck" as we called it back then. We went past my parent's house on a dead end road where no one ever goes. It was after dark and we figured my parents wouldn't even notice we went by the house. We got to the very end of the road and there was my dad, plowing snow! Mike quickly backed up and I prayed we would not go in the ditch and have to have dad plow us out. Whew! That was close.

Next time Mike found a new spot. It was on a little road through a wooded area. I was concerned because it was along a road that my parents passed by a lot, usually on their way to one of those Saturday night dances and he said, "you can't see the car from the road, because of the trees." Okay, we had our fun and the next morning mom asked "what were you and Mike doing parked on that road?" I was mortified and came up with some dumb excuse I am sure. I told Mike, never again!

He did come up with a good idea though. He thought of the gravel pit in Culver. I figured that wasn't a bad idea since mom and dad didn't go that direction too often. Wouldn't you know it, their snowmobile club took a hayride and one of the guys asked, "what's Mike Smith's car doing in the gravel pit?" As this is going on, I am telling Mike "oh no! There goes my dad's tractor and wagon!" Mike's response, "they can't see us from up there." The next day mom stated, "We saw you and Mike last night". I told Mike, "We have got to be the only couple who keeps getting caught by her parents." *I tell you, they must have had built in radar, when it came to me.*

Eventually, Mike got smarter and decided that if we drove down the road next to the railroad tracks in Brookston, there was no way my parents were going to see us. Brilliant! He was right, my parents didn't catch us, but his brother John did. John was a game warden and was parked looking for poachers. Of course, John recognized his brother's car and thought it would be funny to chase us. He never caught us, but it didn't really matter, he knew who was parked in that car.

After months of this, Mike took me out to the dump road and asked me to marry him. Is he a romantic or what! At least, there were no parents or brother. If you are wondering why it was called the dump road, it is just as it sounds. That is where the dump used to be located.

The Honeymoon Is Over

Like any newly married couples, there were adjustments to be made. Mainly, I needed to mold Mike into the perfect husband. I started by refusing to pick his laundry up off the floor. We did our laundry at the Laundromat which was about twenty-five miles away. Mike had this habit of coming in from work and leaving a trail of clothes behind. It was *soooo* annoying. Telling him to pick up after himself, didn't leave any kind of impression on him so I came up with a better idea. I told him "if you don't put your dirty laundry in the hamper, it isn't going to get washed." I went to the Laundromat with the hamper - *not a whole lot of laundry in the hamper*, so I was done faster than usual. Eventually, Mike could not find any clean clothes and questioned me about it. I told him I washed everything that was in the hamper. I could see the light dawn on his face. He was better about picking up after himself after that.

(Late 1979)
Mike's pet peeve about me was when we would go shopping; I always had to think about the item I was planning to buy. The color, size, shape that sort of thing. He told me, "When you go shopping, you need to know what you are going in the store for, get it, pay for it and get out." I decided to do it his way. We needed a file cabinet. I told him, "Okay you pick it out." He walked in, went straight to the file cabinets, knew what size he wanted, got the box down from the shelf, paid for it and got out with a smug

look on his face. I had to give him credit; he was out of the store in record time. We got home, he took it out of the box and his mouth fell open, there was the hot pink file cabinet he picked out all by himself. The smug look was now on my face.

(Early 1980)
Mike has a lot of patience when we go shopping. He will go to the sporting section to kill time and occasionally check to see if I am ready to go yet. If he sees me contemplating the color, size or shape of an item, he'll give me time to come to that decision and may even offer some advice. He really is a wonderful husband!

I practiced motherhood on my sister Robin's kids. She had two toddlers, a boy and a girl. There were times when it was a lot of fun, especially since they eventually went home again.

Our first Valentine's Day, as a married couple, Mike was attending a Police Academy in Utah. I had Robin's three year old son, Nathan, for the day. I told him we were going to make Valentine cookies to send to Uncle Mike. I rolled out the dough and cut out heart shaped cookies. I showed Nathan how to put the cinnamon candies on them. I told him to press the candies onto the cookie just enough so they didn't roll off. He was a quick study. I left him to it and when he was finished we baked them. I wrote to Mike and told him there are cinnamon candies on the cookies but they are on the bottom of the cookies because Nathan wanted to make sure they didn't fall off. They didn't either. Good job Nathan!

I just have to add this story about Nathan too. One spring, he planted vegetable seeds and *every day* during the summer, he would check to see if they were growing yet. He must have been about sixteen then, not really, he was only about four or five. My sister and I knew that he wasn't going to get anything, so I came up with an idea. I brought a pumpkin and some other vegetables and put them in his garden. When Nathan checked his garden he was amazed to see all the vegetables he had grown. He was a proud boy that day. Hopefully, I haven't burst his bubble, because I don't know if we ever did tell him the truth, but he can probably handle it now that he is about thirty years old.

Mike and I had an opportunity to practice being parents together. My sister Robin's daughter Kristie was a little over a year old when Robin asked if I wanted to baby sit for a weekend. I thought it would be fun! I was *so naïve*. We took Kristie with us to my parent's house, but they weren't home. We went in to use the phone and while I was on the phone, Kristie crawled onto a dining room chair and got stuck between the back rest and the seat of the chair. I panicked because I could not get her out. Her head was too big to fit. I could just imagine handing the chair and baby to my sister and hoping she wouldn't notice. No matter how hard I tried that head was not going to fit through the opening. Mike came up with an idea, "why not pull her out the other way, because her stomach is more flexible." *Must have been how she got in there in the first place.* We got her out and I told Mike, "WE ARE NEVER HAVING KIDS!" Several months later we had Michael and three more kids after that.

When I was pregnant with our first son, Mike was gone to the Police Academy for three months in Utah. I had my sister Gayle stay with me once in awhile. She was about five. I suffered from morning sickness and Charlie horses in both hips. Every morning without fail, I would wake up, get out of bed and run to the bathroom before the Charlie horses had a chance to kick in. I would be throwing up and hanging onto the sink for dear life as the Charlie horses started. After this was all over I would take my iron pill.

Gayle witnessed this routine one morning. After I took the pill she said, "Susan I know what that pill is for." I replied, "You do?" Gayle said, "Yeah, it's so you don't have a baby." I thought to myself, *I better quit taking it then because I sure don't want to be pregnant the rest of my life the way I'm feeling now.*

My sister Brenda has three kids and they are the only ones I haven't mentioned from my side of the family. I tried to come up with a *humorous story* about them but "I got nothing." Suffice to say, their names are Timmy, Cody and Katie. Timmy and Cody are the boys and Katie is the girl, which means she has two sons and one daughter.

We didn't always get to see the kids, because their parents had joint custody and often the family events were on the opposite times that Brenda had them. Timmy joined the army - *not funny;* Cody will soon graduate from high school - YAHOO! And Katie just got her driver's license, AAAAAAAAH!!!!!!!

Family, Family And More Family

In the earlier years, Mike was a little on the shy side. Those were the good old days. He was always respectful and didn't like to be rude to my parents. It was hard to get used to my family, as they were a little on the quiet side themselves. Okay, okay that is a flat out lie about my family! However, they can be quiet, usually when they are sleeping.

Anyway, my mother loved to make Tapioca. It is a comfort food we really enjoy. When we are feeling down, Tapioca is sure to lift the spirits. After I had back surgery my mother made it for me, it was the only thing that tasted good, everything else nauseated me. In other words, there is just no better food than Tapioca. You would NEVER think of throwing it behind a dresser.

Mom figured everyone must feel the same way about Tapioca as we do. Mike and I were visiting and she made a huge pot of Tapioca. She always gave generous helpings too. She set a nice big soup bowl full of the stuff on the table in front of Mike. He smiled and thanked her and I tried not to laugh, because I knew Mike detested Tapioca. I chose not to help him out on this one. He very politely ate it. Mom offered him more and he very politely declined. Well, mom wasn't having any of that, he was just being polite and she just knew he really wanted more. She said, "oh come on, have some more" and proceeded to fill that bowl up a second time! He ate it too! You won't catch him being that polite anymore. Now he tells her, I'm on my way over, put the damn coffee pot on. Of course, she knows he's kidding, so when he gets there she tells him, "Here's your damn coffee." Can't you just feel the love?

When Mike and I first started dating, my little sister Gayle who was about four years old at the time, took a real shine to Mike. Before we could go out, Mike would have to sit and hold her on his lap until she fell asleep and then carry her to bed. She did not want to be left out, *ever*.

One time, Mike and I decided to take a walk along the railroad tracks near my parent's house. Gayle wanted to tag along; I told her "not this time." She figured she would follow anyway. I looked behind me and there she was coming down the hill as fast as her little legs could carry her. I told her to go back and she screamed at me "I HATE YOU SUSAN!" That's the kind of treatment I get from the little girl who would wait for me to come home from my night job. She would be standing in the kitchen and ask me "Ufee will you make me some Malt-O-Meal?" She couldn't say Susie. I made Malt-o-meal for this little girl every morning, whether I felt like it or not. That girl loved breakfast. She ate it with Dad, me and then again when our other sisters went to school. She was also the little girl that I had to rock to sleep every night. It had to be me, apparently it was my job and I did it. Now, she tells me she hates me! That is what happens when sisters like the same guy. The fact that I was fourteen years older than her really didn't play into it at all. Everything turned out fine, she was in the wedding, but as the flower girl, I got to be the bride.

Mike had a nephew the same age as Gayle. His nickname was "Winky." I don't why, but it was. Anyway, Mike informed me that Winky did not like me at all because I had taken his uncle Mike away. Apparently, I was not popular with that age group. They're very competitive at that age; when it comes to Mike anyway. I dreaded meeting him for the first time, but he was respectful, if a little distant.

Mike really had me convinced Winky would never accept me. Winky was the ring bearer in the wedding, he didn't try to sabotage it in any way, so I figured that was progress.

The first Mother's Day, after we were married, there was a knock on the door. There stood Winky and his cousin Amanda with wildflowers in their hands. They said "here, Happy Mother's Day" and left. It was then that I realized he accepted me and he never did say "I HATE YOU SUSAN!" unlike some youngster.

When I met Mike's family, my first impression was, they were nothing like mine, and they were a lot quieter. First impressions can be so deceiving. His family was HUGE! I don't mean physically, there were a lot of them. *I really need to be careful how I word things.* Mike has five sisters and one brother and they have families of their own, anywhere from two to five kids each. His parents were small and I have no idea where these big sons of theirs came from. I am sure his mom, Dottie, would have liked *not* to lay claim to them at times, but the resemblance was definitely there.

Mike's Dad, Art, was very quiet and I didn't get to know him as well as I would have liked. He died after Mike and I had been married only a couple of years. One memory really stands out in my mind. He loved his Alaskan Husky, "Baby." The dog was gorgeous and very big. As I mentioned before, Mike's dad wasn't a big man and when he took his dog for a walk, it was really hard to determine, who was walking whom. I saw "Baby" pulling Art through a ditch. *Man*! That guy could run when he didn't have any choice! Luckily, the dog knew his way home or we may never have known what became of Art.

The day Art died, everyone gathered at Dottie's house after we left the hospital. It was my first real experience with how Mike's family coped in a crisis. I figured everyone would sit around reminiscing about the good times, maybe shed a few tears. How wrong I was. The minute Mike's sisters walked into the house, the cleaning supplies came out. They proceeded to clean the house. My brain did not quite function that way; I was in more of a fog than anything. However, I figured if I was going to fit into this family, I better buck up and start cleaning. Dusting doesn't take a lot of thought, so I opted to do that.

I got the can of dusting spray and a cloth out of the cupboard. As I was dusting I had an awful time getting it to spray out of the can the right way. Instead of coming out the side it came out the top of the can. I worked with it anyway. After I was all done, I told the family the problem I had with the can and as I was telling the story of the faulty can, I looked at it and realized I had dusted all the furniture with air freshener! Of course, they all knew it too and my brother-in-law Tom said, "It sure smells good in here." Nice thing to say, but how much you want to bet he was thinking *"what an idiot, I wonder what she uses to clean the toilet bowl?"* Who would ever guess, that as I got older, cleaning and decorating would be my main stress reliever. I am now the queen of the stress-relieving cleaning.

Mike's mom Dottie and I shared many laughs. My favorite story about her involves her grand-daughter. We lived across the road from Dottie and I walked over to visit. Her grand-daughter, Tara was visiting. She must have been about three at the time. This red-headed little girl was very busy. She came out of the entry way by the kitchen door with her fists clenched together. Dottie said to her "what do you have? Give it to Grandma." Tara, doing as she was told gave it to her. Dottie's next words were, "IT'S CAT SHIT, YOU ISHY, ISHY GIRL!" The litter box was kept in the entry way. I sat there ready to laugh and Dottie shook her finger at me and said "AND DON'T YOU LAUGH!" I really tried not to, the tears were streaming down my face, but I wasn't laughing. Finally, she noticed how I was struggling not to laugh and she broke down and laughed herself. I said to her, "you told her to give it to you." We were both crying with laughter.

Dottie loved to bake and she and I decided to try this new recipe that her oldest daughter Joan gave her. They were Mounds Bars. Some of the main ingredients were instant potatoes, coconut and powdered sugar. We carefully measured all the ingredients, but as we mixed them, we both had puzzled expressions on our faces. How are they going to stick together? The only liquid in them was vanilla. We thought about adding water, but we were afraid we would ruin it. Mike's sister Linda came in and we asked her; she didn't know she had never made them before. Dottie and I still tried to figure it out and we finally, gave up and I called Joan.

She went down the list of ingredients and I assured her we had it all in there, but the balls didn't stick together. Exasperated, she asked "did you cook the potatoes first?" Sheepishly, I told her "I guess that must be the problem." Dottie and I never lived that one down.

Dottie moved down the road to a smaller house. Her youngest daughter, Terri and I started moving her, *Dottie's possessions*, that is. She wouldn't get on the dolly and let us put her in the back of the truck. We loaded up what we could in Terri's truck and brought it down to the new house. After we unloaded the first load, we were on our way back up the hill for another, when we looked off into the woods and noticed there was a mattress hanging in the trees. That's odd we thought. Who would throw a mattress in the trees? That was when we realized, THAT'S MOM'S/DOTTIE'S MATTRESS! We pulled over, crawled through the ditch and rescued it. My thought now is, *just how fast was Terri driving?* We got Dottie moved and as far as I know, we didn't decorate anymore trees with her possessions.

My fondest memories are of Christmas Eve. We always had dinner at Dottie's house. It didn't matter we were wall to wall people. We stood up eating, leaning against cupboards, walls and anything else we could find. There was always plenty of laughter and oh how Mike could tease his mother. He is great for name calling and loved to call her a "Banty Hen." She would walk up to him and swat him with a dish towel. Christmas Eve has never been the same since she passed away, but what wonderful memories we all have.

My Three Sons

Mike and I started a family right away. Our first son was born after we had been married eleven months. Mike has dark brown hair and is ¼ Native American and has German in him. I am a strawberry blonde, at least I used to be, and I am Irish, Swedish, Norwegian, English, in other words, Heinz 57 as Mike likes to point out.

Our first son, Michael was a summer baby. During my pregnancy, my hair had bleached out in the sun and I was a golden blonde. I went into labor on the fourth of July and gave birth to him on the fifth. As his head appeared the nurses exclaimed "he has red hair!" They laughed and looked at mine and Mike's hair and asked "where did the red hair come from doctor?" We all looked at the doctor's full head of red hair and laughed.

Michael loved to go riding in the International Scout with his dad. They were going somewhere when all of a sudden a squirrel came up by the gear shift. Michael spotted it and started yelling "KANGAROO, KANGAROO!" I don't think he has ever seen a kangaroo since, but he has seen plenty of squirrels.

Michael had his own vocabulary. I never quite figured out where these words came from, but he would call the basement "ding a ding," water was "ning a ning," and my cousin Mary was "Mingo." Of course, Mike and I went along with it and the next thing we knew, we were going to the "ding a ding" and drinking "ning a ning." Michael eventually learned the English language and never stopped talking.

My sister, April offered to baby sit. I warned her he likes to talk, a lot. She didn't mind, she wanted to take him to town with her. After they came back, she had a glazed look in her eyes and said, "He never stops talking!" I tried to tell her.

Michael was about three or four years old, when we went to visit April. At that time she and her husband were in the process of building a house and were temporarily living in the basement. April had been next door, swimming in her in-law's swimming pool. She decided to take her suit off in the laundry room since she was home alone and then go to the bathroom to shower. As she went around the corner to the bathroom which was on the way to the stairs leading into the basement, she encountered Michael. They both stopped cold, with their mouths gapping open; eventually April did move and got dressed.

As we were visiting, April asked, "Does Michael ever see you naked?" I thought *what an odd question*. I had no idea where she was going with that, but I humored her and told her "no." She said "well, he saw me naked." She explained what happened so I had some warning, if Michael said anything. We were on our way home in the car when Michael hesitantly said "mom?" I said "what," and as *fast* as he could say it he said "I saw April and she was NAKED!" I guess he had quite an education that day, thanks to April I never had to explain the differences between the male and female body.

Michael loved to dance. At a Christmas party at the Legion - yes, even the kids went in on occasion. There was a Christmas dance. The music was playing on the juke box and Michael could be seen dancing every dance with a frilly pink lamp shade on his head. You can still find him dancing, minus the lamp shade; at least I hope so, down at the same bar.

Marshall was born less than two years after Michael. He was born in December. As I mentioned before, Mike is Native American and when Marshall was born it came out. He looked like Mike's mother. He had dark hair and complexion. As he got older his hair turned blonde and eventually a lighter shade of brown.

Marshall was a busy child. One day, my mother-in-law called from across the street and asked, "What kind of lights do you have *on* over there." From where she was, it looked like we had one of those balls you find in a dance hall that give off little flecks of light. I had to tell her "Marshall climbed up on the table and was swinging from the chandelier." Sad to say, she wasn't surprised when it came to Marshall. There were five globes on that chandelier and they were all barely hanging on, but by some stroke of luck, none of them got broken.

Marshall was always fascinated with tools. One day, I came up from the "ding a ding" I mean basement, when Marshall showed me his handy work. He found a screwdriver and took all the electrical plates off the walls in the hallway. HE WAS ONLY FOUR YEARS OLD! Luckily, he did not get electrocuted.

Whenever, Mike was working on one of our vehicles, Marshall was right there to watch. One day Mike left the hood up on our International Scout. Marshall came strutting through the kitchen with a handful of tools and said "I'll fix it!" I yelled to Mike, "MARSHALL IS ON HIS WAY OUT SIDE TO FIX THE SCOUT!" Mike went running out the door.

Marshall liked the sound of breaking glass. He discovered that if you threw a baseball at the basement window it made a really cool sound. His dad didn't think so. Marshall took one look at his dad's face and ran for the house - he didn't have picnic woods. He locked the door and stood there looking at his dad through the window. Mike angrily told him "OPEN THE DOOR!" Marshall calmly nodded his head no. Smart kid!

Marshall had a few stays in the hospital, due to pneumonia. As he started to feel better the nursing staff didn't know quite how to keep him safe anymore. They had him in a metal crib with bars much taller than he was and he still got out. Finally, they had to put the bars over the top, as well, which they hated to do because he looked like he was in a cage. The staff was happy to discharge him into our care!

Marshall was the kid always getting stitches or breaking something. He broke both wrists by standing on a see saw while another child held the other end and sent him airborne. Marshall came down on both wrists. Of course, he did this shortly before his younger brother had hip surgery. I had one kid with both wrists in slings and casts and the other in a wheelchair with both legs in casts. It did not look good for me when I took them out in public, which I tried to avoid as much as possible. Would you believe this still didn't slow Marshall down!

Marshall had a hard time pronouncing certain words. Mike would call him "Bucko." I told Mike he couldn't call him that anymore because Marshall was calling other people that and it wasn't' coming out the same, it started with an "F."

My sister-in-law would baby sit for me a lot and Marshall just loved her, he took to calling her ma and I was "hey you." Warms the heart, doesn't it? I could go on and on about Marshall's escapades through the years, but that is a book in itself.

Mitchell was born in October. He was a big baby, almost ten pounds! It felt like it too! It was natural childbirth all the way. He is the one that gave me hemorrhoids. He can still be a real pain in the - never mind.

I'll never forget when he was being born; the nurses exclaimed "it's a beautiful baby!" I had visions of a baby with lots of dark hair and a beautiful complexion. *Wrong.* Mitchell was born sunny side up which means, face up rather than down. He was really white and had red circles around his eyes. The doctor laid him on my stomach and I turned to Mike and said "this has got to be the homeliest baby I ever saw." Mike scolded me and said "that's your son you're talking about." I replied, "I love him anyway, I can't help it he looks like a raccoon." After a few hours the red spots faded and he got some color in his face. He really was adorable.

The nursing staff was a little concerned the first day, because he hadn't been able to urinate yet. That is the *professional* name for pee. They didn't want to worry me, but decided they would have to mention it. I walked down to the nursery to check on my baby, on hearing this. As I approached the nursery, there was a lot of activity going on, the nurses were shoving babies in bassinettes away and standing back from the one in the middle which held my baby boy. He no longer had a peeing problem; he really let fly and everyone near must have felt they were in a rain storm. There were wet nurses and babies and they did not do it to themselves. THAT'S MY BOY! I may have exaggerated the rain storm a bit, but *doggone it*, I was so proud!

When Mitchell was two years old, he became very ill. He was lethargic and wasn't able to stand up. Mike and I rushed him to the hospital. They tested him for meningitis, Ryes Syndrome, among other things. He was slipping into a coma and we still didn't know what was wrong. All they could treat him for was a throat infection and hepatitis. They knew there was more wrong, but after cat scans and every blood test they could come up with, they determined it had to be encephalomyelitis. It was a form of encephalitis which is an inflammation of the brain caused by a viral infection. The myelititis was the paralysis he had from it.

In the early 80s, there was no test to determine this disease. The doctors had to rule out other diseases to make the diagnosis. Many years later, specialists were able to do a muscle biopsy during one of his many surgeries and determine that he had had encephalomyeloradiculitis which is an inflammation of the brain, spinal cord and spinal roots. Amazing how far medical science has come in such a short time. Now there is treatment as well as a way to test for it. Now if they could just figure out a way to name these diseases so we can pronounce them that would be awesome.

Getting back to when Mitchell was in the hospital, we were told he had a 50/50 chance of surviving. If he did survive, there could be many complications: mental retardation, paralysis, vegetative state etc. Eventually, he came out of his coma. The main complication Mitchell encountered was paralysis. There was no mental retardation and the paralysis over time would greatly improve with years of therapy and operations.

One day I walked into Mitchell's room and a male nurse was trying to feed him. People, who come out of comas, often come out angry - *that* would be Mitchell. The nurse was doing the whole airplane trick trying to get Mitchell to eat. I stood in the doorway and watched for awhile. The nurse was very animated in his efforts to get Mitchell to eat. Mitchell just glared at him. At this point the nurse spotted me and in a very relieved tone said "oh good mom's here. You know if you could bottle that killer look, you would make a fortune." What the nurse didn't know was that look was in Mitchell's family genes. I took over from there and he *did* eat.

The pediatricians came in. They were a husband and wife team. The husband checked down Mitchell's throat. He put his fingers in Mitchell's mouth. BIG MISTAKE! Mitchell clamped down and there was no getting him to let loose. I swear that boy is part pit bull. I was mortified and scolding Mitchell to let go while the wife of the team was laughing. Mitchell drew blood and the doctor was not laughing, but his wife still was.

She scolded him for not knowing better than to put his fingers in Mitchell's mouth. Who knew that Mitchell would become one of the easiest going people you could ever hope to meet.

He has had several hip surgeries, ham string lengthening, botox shots and countless therapy over the years. His first surgery involved breaking both hips and rotating them. The first time, as Mike and I waited with him to go into surgery, he looked at us and said "there's something wrong with my knees, they keep knocking." He didn't understand it was because he was so nervous.

When Mitchell was about three years old, he loved to play hide and seek. One of my cousins came to visit. After drinking too much Diet Coke, she needed to use the restroom. She was sitting on the toilet when off to her right, Mitchell whipped open the shower curtain and shouted "SURPRISE!" My cousin told me, she was sure glad he waited until she was sitting before he surprised her.

In spite of all the health problems Mitchell had, he always maintained his good humor and enjoyment of life. Maybe, once in awhile he would not maintain his good humor. If he was told "no," he would stomp his foot and say "I'm nothing!" He would stomp down the hallway, slam the door and stay in his room. I never had to send him to his room, he was already there and *ooooh the peace and quiet.*

As Mitchell got older, he and I formed a special bond; one that most mothers and sons would probably not want to have. Mitchell had multiple surgeries and so did I.

I had back surgeries the last of which two fusions were done. One fusion was done with bone from a cadaver which I am grateful for, but *so* do not want to think too much about. The other was done with a rod. I also had a cage inserted through my stomach - no I don't have any songbirds in there, however that may explain why I cannot sing very well - Mike would probably think there is a parrot in there that never shuts up, but *really* it isn't that kind of cage. It replaces one of the discs. I had degenerative disease so things were not going so well in there. I am doing great now though - best thing I ever did was have that surgery, right up there with getting married and having kids - painful but worth it!

Getting back to why I bring this up, both Mitchell and I had difficulty keeping up with everyone else when we were on vacation. We went to Mount Rushmore, *it's in South Dakota.* We did a lot of walking which was no easy feat for me and Mitchell. We would look at each other and one would ask, "Are you thinking about sitting on the bench over there?" The other would respond, "I will, if you will." We had our dignity to preserve.

Because of all that Mitchell has endured, he has empathy for others and is often approached as someone safe to talk to about personal problems. People sense that Mitchell will not judge them harshly.

Boys Will Be Boys

My three sons could get into plenty of trouble individually, but put them all together and watch out!

Michael and Marshall went missing one time. I frantically, searched the yard and all over the house. They were not allowed to cross the road alone, but they loved going to "Nonnie's" house and she always gave them fruit. I figured they may have sneaked across the road so I picked up the phone to call my mother-in-law, when who should appear "not eight tiny reindeer" but my two missing sons. Each one had an apple in one hand and an orange in the other. *They were caught or so I thought.* I asked "where did you get those apples and oranges?" With Michael being the clever boy that he was, he piped up with, "off the trees in the backyard." I thought to myself, now *let me see, we live in Northern Minnesota, not Sunny, Florida, what are the chances those came off of our trees?* FAT CHANCE OF THAT HAPPENING! Nice try Michael, but you are in *sooooo* much trouble!

My sons had a creative streak in them too. They were not allowed to go outside in the morning until I got up. Yes, with three boys in the house I was tired and liked to sleep in when I could. They were good about sticking to this rule. One morning they must have thought to themselves *it sure would be nice to have roads for our matchbox cars to drive through, but we are not allowed to go out to the sandbox by ourselves, what can we do? I know! There's a lot of flour and sugar and a whole kitchen floor to use.* And that is just what they did. What a mess!

Mitchell recalls a time that my sisters and I were visiting our parents along with our children. The boys came up with a great idea, at least two of them did. I believe it was Michael and my nephew Daniel, clever Robin's son. They thought they would cut a few small trees down for Grandpa. Grandpa however was not impressed. Grandpa planted those trees and liked having them in the ground. He lectured those boys and when he was through with them, he came into the house and lectured the mothers, much to the delight of the boys, until the mothers got hold of them.

My boys grew up with lots of cousins on both sides of the family and what one doesn't think of doing one of the others are sure to come up with an idea. My niece Tara was a little older than Michael. Actually, she still is. Michael has never been able to pass her up, because every year he has a birthday, she has one too. She and Michael were sitting at a children's round table pretending to have tea and gossiping. Kids! I don't know where they get these ideas. Anyway, Tara had an idea that I can't recall what it was, but I remember Michael's response, "we can't because mom will find out and SHE KNOWS EVERYTHING!"

He really believed this because when the three boys would take a bath, they could not figure out how I could be in the dining room on the phone and still know what they were doing. What they did not know was I had a mirror on the hallway wall directly across from the bathroom. I could look in that mirror, see into the bathroom mirror which was across from the bathtub and see everything they were doing.

Over the years, I sure wish I could have figured out a way to have mirrors around them at all times, because somewhere along the line, they figured out, mom *doesn't* know everything.

Foster Children

For a brief time before Mitchell was born, we decided to have foster children. I really wanted to have a little girl in the house. We ended up taking in a two year old boy and a three year old girl. I'll call them "Mickey and Minnie." Alright, I know that isn't very clever, but it works.

Mickey was in diapers along with Michael and Marshall. They each had their own of course, we didn't make them share. Minnie was potty trained. We took them all on a trip to visit a friend in Missouri and what a trip it was! We would stop at wayside rests, Mike would take Minnie to the bathroom and I would line up all the others like they were on an assembly line to change their diapers. Needless to say, a lot of looks were sent my way.

Mickey was Native American and had very dark hair and skin. Michael was a redhead with freckles and Marshall by then had blonde hair. They were the cutest bunch, but they did not look anything alike. Out of the bathroom came Minnie who also had dark hair, but wasn't quite as dark skinned as her brother. People would question me and ask "are those yours?" I was tempted to mess with their minds and say "that one is mine, I kidnapped that one and the other two followed me home one day and I figured what the heck I might as well keep them too." I figured they may not recognize the sarcastic tone and I would wind up in jail - not a place I was wanting to tour on that particular trip. That would be a trip in itself.

Minnie was quite a challenge. When she lived with us, we did not know about Fetal Alcohol Syndrome, which is caused by the mother drinking alcohol while she was pregnant, causing brain damage to the fetus. Studies show that it could possibly be caused by the father's drinking, as well.

Minnie was one you had to repeat instructions to, over and over again. One time in particular, the kids were playing in the yard. I was cleaning house. Minnie knocked on the door because she couldn't open it herself. I opened the door and she told me she wanted water. I got her some water and she went back to play. Not two minutes later she was on the door again. She had to go potty. She took care of business and went back outside. A couple of minutes later she came to the door to tattle on one of the other kids. I told her to quit knocking on the door and go play. I barely walked away and there's that knock again. By then I was really fed up! I flung open the door and shouted "WHAT DO YOU WANT NOW?" I stopped in shock; there stood one of Mike's partners from work looking just as shocked as I was. In a small voice I said, "oh hi," like he wasn't going to notice that I had just yelled at him. He stated his business and left. Funny thing, he would call before stopping by after that.

Eventually, Mickey and Minnie moved on to another foster home. I don't think it was located in Florida or California. That was a different Mickey and Minnie.

Tragedy Strikes

Before Mitchell became ill, Mike and I had decided to adopt a little girl. We filled out all the paperwork, *which is the labor part when adopting.* We were put on the waiting list.

After Mitchell started recovering, we thought about the adoption and decided the sex of the baby didn't seem quite as important anymore as long as the baby was healthy. We decided to have one more biologically. We called our social worker and asked her to remove our names from the waiting list. It didn't take long and we were expecting. We were excited and the boys called him "Baby Chris." Like the first baby, this one was due on the 4th of July again.

I was sick throughout the entire pregnancy and bled a lot. The doctor could find nothing wrong. The baby's heartbeat was strong and he kicked a lot. By the time I entered the fifth month and went in for my regular check-up, I knew something was terribly wrong. The doctor could no longer hear the heartbeat and I did not feel movement anymore. An ultrasound was performed and it was determined the baby had died. I was told to go home and wait for either labor to begin or for my uterus to shrink and then I could have a D&C. We were devastated! It took three weeks for my uterus to shrink, but at last I was able to have the D&C.

Before surgery, I told Mike to make sure the funeral home was called. I wanted to bury the baby and we had already made the arrangements before hand. I had a feeling I wouldn't be able to ensure this was done. I was right!

After I was brought to the recovery room, I began to hemorrhage. As I came out of the anesthesia, I saw the nurses and doctors rushing around and shoving another stretcher out of the way. I remember thinking, *why are they shoving that poor patient away?* It was then I realized that I was bleeding massively. When I realized there was a chance I wouldn't pull through, I said to the anesthesiologist, who was sitting right by my head, "if you think I am slipping away, remind me that Marshall really needs me."

The reason I felt Marshall needed me the most was because I had been advocating for services to help lay the ground work for his education later on. Marshall's hearing loss had gone undetected in the beginning. I felt he had hearing loss and had him tested. While he was in surgery having tubes put in his ears, a test was performed. The results of this test were sent away to specialists to read. They read them wrong! We lost two years before an audiologist doing routine testing at head start caught it. Don't you just love it when "specialists" know more about your kid than you do?

I had been the one laying the ground work with a school district that was less than enthused. The battle with the school district would be an ongoing process but luckily we had the law on our side. Mike didn't have the opportunity to learn what those laws were and I hadn't kept him as informed as I should have. I learned my lesson there, and later kept Mike better informed. I mention this, only because all my kids were equally important in my life, and still are, unless I am mad at one of them, then maybe not so much, but I was in the middle of some major stuff that could affect the rest of Marshall's life. It was not a good time for me to "check out."

The staff was pumping blood into both arms. I depleted their blood supply and they called another hospital nearby for more. *I was kind of gluttonous when it came to that blood.* There was no time to warm it up, so they pumped it into my arms cold and it wasn't a slow drip either. It kind of felt like one of those "ice-cream" headaches, except in both arms and it was not over in seconds. My blood pressure would go too high and then drop too low. I felt like I was lying on a seesaw, they would practically stand me on my head, and then I would have to go the opposite direction. I was cold, and then I was hot. My arms felt like someone was trying to rip them off of me. At that point, I almost wished someone would. My stomach felt as though a semi-truck were parked on it.

I prayed to God. *"Oh God, please don't let me die today, Marshall needs me, but if I'm going to get Aids from all the blood then take me now."* I could not watch or read the news, for a year after this happened because the Aid's epidemic was at the height of its publicity.

The pain was intense, and then all of a sudden, there was no pain. I felt light weight and could see a bright round light. I started toward it. I felt euphoric until I heard a voice in my ear, "hang in there Susan, Marshall still needs you." It wasn't God, it was the anesthesiologist. I began to fight and all of a sudden the pain came slamming back into my body. It was not a gradual process which made the pain harder to tolerate. Going from feeling "light as a feather" to feeling like the semi-truck had landed again - only this time it was dropped on me.

A doctor appeared and he asked me, "Susan, how many of me do you see?" I said, "Two." He laughed and replied, "That's too many of me to have to look at." In spite of all he had to do he maintained his humor and made me laugh, even though it hurt. Two more times I saw that light and felt light-weight and I heard that voice remind me about Marshall needing me and each time was harder to come back to that intense pain.

In the middle of all this drama, Mike was told to be prepared; the odds were against me to pull through this. My family and Mike's family were called to the hospital. One of the doctors told Mike to go into the room to see me, but to smile and not let on anything was wrong. *I had a pretty good idea, things weren't going well when I looked down at the end of the stretcher and the blood was pooling on the floor and the staff had no time to clean it up, so they threw towels on it temporarily. The fact that I wasn't feeling well gave me another clue.*

Anyway, they let Mike in to see me. What I did not know was my lips were blue as well as my fingers. Blue *isn't* one of my best colors. Just as Mike walked into the room, I threw up. He smiled at me just as he was told, turned around and walked back out. That isn't the effect Mike usually has on me, I can usually hold down my lunch. Mike later told me, when he saw what shape I was in, he walked out and broke down sobbing. He did well though - he smiled at me - too bad I had disgusting fluids coming out both ends. I might have been able to smile back.

Somewhere along the line, I was diagnosed as having an amniotic fluid embolism. The amniotic fluid had dripped into my blood stream which prevented the blood from clotting. I developed multiple complications from it and the doctor of Internal Medicine later told me that it was so intense; he finally had to prioritize each complication and figure out how to treat each one. The man is a genius; I am still here today with no problems resulting from that time. I later found out my chances for survival were ten percent.

In the middle of all this drama, Mike remembered what I said about the baby. Luckily, he did because the staff didn't remember the funeral home was coming for him. They would have taken care of the fetus, as the professionals called him, because I was only five months along when this happened.

After twenty-three pints of blood I was stabilized enough to be brought to the Intensive Care Unit. Family, were able to take turns coming in to see me. I wasn't out of the woods yet, but I was alive. I had congestive heart failure and was told I needed a Swan Ganz Catheter inserted through my neck and down to my heart. I was scared. I asked, "I have to be awake for this?" The nurse told me, "It isn't as bad as it sounds."

A nurse put a towel over my face so when the blood spurted out after the doctor made the incision, I would not have it in my face. I told the nurse, "I can't breathe." She replied, "I don't know why not, you have an oxygen mask on." Well, that's beside the point. Then she stated, "I think someone is a little claustrophobic." I am pretty sure she meant me. The procedure really wasn't as bad as it sounded.

The next day, my little sister Gayle was coming to see me. With all the equipment I was hooked up to; there were several I.V. drips inserted in my arms and several monitors beeping and my family felt she would be upset or frightened by the way I looked. I suspect she probably was even before this happened. They prepared her the best they could and I decided I would be as cheerful for her benefit as I could, after seeing how the older sisters reacted - *crying and carrying on something awful like they really cared.* I figured this would be very traumatic for Gayle. She walked in, sat down and said "Susan, you look like a duck." So much for being traumatized! The oxygen mask I had on did look like a duck's bill.

My three sons came to visit me. Michael was inquisitive, wanting to know what everything was. Marshall was having a hard time understanding what happened and was frightened by all the equipment. *Apparently he wasn't seeing a cute little duck.* After talking to him, he recognized his mother under all that equipment and crawled into the bed

69

with me. Mitchell was too young to really grasp the situation at all.

Christopher was buried in Culver Cemetery while I was in the coronary care unit. My sister's-in-law Rozanne and Lois, came to be with me while the graveside service was being performed.

In retrospect…As I was editing this section it suddenly occurred to me that when I wrote, about the anesthesiologist talking to me and I said that it wasn't God - I am sure now that it was. Over the years I have recalled that voice in my ear and I assumed it was the anesthesiologist because I had asked him to remind me "Marshall needs me" and I am sure that he did do this, but what puzzled me all these years, is how I heard him so clearly and I do have hearing loss as well as the trauma I was in at the time.

This has been quite a revelation. I have not put as much deep thought into what happened as I did, writing this. It was one of the sections I most dreaded writing about because I did not want to get sucked into that dark tunnel of despair again. Who would have thought it would be the most rewarding part of the whole book. A feeling of peace has come over me as I write this and I think of my favorite poem, written by Mary Stevenson.

Footprints In The Sand

On night I dreamed I was walking
Along the beach with the Lord.
Many scenes from my life flashed across the sky.
In each scene I noticed footprints in the sand…

If you have never read this poem before, it is well worth looking up in the library or on the web. It would be even better to buy it in picture form and have it accessible during those times when life gets you down. It is sure to bring you comfort.

I have read this poem many times and have several copies all over the house. It truly has helped remind me that God is always with us. How I managed to over-look the fact that he was in the room with me through one of the most harrowing times in my life, I'll never understand.

A Miracle

As time went on, Mike and I really felt the loss of the baby. The doctor strongly suggested not having anymore babies because it would be risky. We regretted telling our social worker to take us off the adoption list. We decided to start over and contact our social worker and start the paperwork again.

We found out that the social worker we had before, had been promoted about the time we called and asked her to remove our names from the list. After checking on our last paperwork, it was discovered that our names had never been taken off the list! God *does* work in mysterious ways.

We made one change in the paperwork. It no longer mattered if it were a boy or a girl.

It's A Girl!

In a few short months, our new social worker contacted us. They had a two year old girl for us and we were told her name was Kristin. We traveled to St. Paul to meet with her social worker and to meet our little girl for the first time. We met at the social services building and learned more. We were told she was *eighteen months old* and her name was *Krystal*. I don't think I have ever met anyone who got younger rather than older as Krystal did.

We drove to the foster home and met Krystal. She was very tiny; she looked like she was only about nine months old. She had dark brown hair and beautiful brown eyes. She was of Native American and Asian descent - still is, for that matter.

We arranged to come back the following weekend with the boys. We were to stay at a motel and spend the weekend together. That was the longest week of our lives! The boys met her for the first time and she flung herself at them. She was a little hard to contain at that point. We had a great time and the next weekend she came to live with us. We were asked what we wanted to name her. I felt that her name was all she had to bring with her so we changed the spelling of her first name to K-r-y-s-t-l-e and her middle name to my middle name and my mother's first name, Diane. She did not have to get used to being called by an unfamiliar name.

Krystle had one word she would say, "Yody, yody, yody." As we became more familiar with her, we discovered it meant, dirty. She hated getting her hands dirty, which meant we were constantly washing her hands.

I was in "seventh heaven," shopping for girl things. I bought her a pair of red shoes. She loved those shoes. Anytime someone would talk to her, she would look down at her feet and point at her red shoes. Now that I think about it, maybe she thought she could do like Dorothy in the "Wizard of Oz" and click those together three times and go back to where she came from. If that were the case, it didn't work because she was stuck with us and we were off on our roller coaster ride.

Raising Krystle

As Krystle grew, we started noticing her behavior wasn't always typical of other children her age. She would have the usual temper tantrums that other children have, except hers were more extreme. She would scream and carry on for hours. She did this at Grandma Dottie's house one time. Dottie took one look at Krystle, shook her finger at her and said "you ishy ishy girl, acting like that at Grandma's house." Krystle stopped! I don't know what magic that woman had in her finger, but that was the end of those awful tantrums. I told Dottie, "I sure wish you had done that weeks ago."

When Krystle was about three years old, we took her to a clinic to find out if she had Fetal Alcohol Syndrome. After all the tests were done it was suspected she may have Fetal Alcohol Effect, which is the same thing but without the physical characteristics. As she got older we would know more.

Krystle was a joy, but I gotta tell you, watching T.V. with her was like trying to watch two shows with her being the star attraction in one of them. She would lie on the floor in front of the set and the whole time she would be moving. She was so flexible that she would wrap her legs around her neck and that is no exaggeration. It was like a one person wrestling match! No wonder to this day she loves to watch wrestling.

When she entered Kindergarten, the teacher would tell us what a smart girl she was, however she did her best to irritate other children - *Krystle*, not the teacher. She would tap her fingers on the table, if she got no reaction, she would move just a tad closer, still no reaction, she was practically in the kids face, PLENTY OF REACTION THEN! She could not understand why the other child would hit her. Go figure!

She and her brothers would really get into some battles. She was relentless in whatever it was she chose to do to torment them. She always singled one out and he would be the target for weeks! Oh lucky, lucky boy!

That "Hansen Look" that people would cower from? NOT KRYSTLE! She would push past that fine line you never cross with your parents. The line children know by reading their parents body language and know when to back off.

It was many years later Krystle and I had a discussion about reading a person's body language. I talked to her about how everyone has something about them that gives a clue when they are very angry. I explained about in my family, our eyes are that clue, the dreaded "Hansen Look." She had absolutely no idea what I was talking about. What a blow to the ego! I thought that "Hansen Look" could fix anything - one of those rare occasions I was wrong!

As Krystle entered into puberty, *what is the phrase I am looking for?* ALL HELL BROKE LOOSE! She was much more sophisticated in her tormenting of people. Being her mother, I was her primary target. Of course, being around her peers, they unwittingly fed into it. Some of her peer's parents did as well. I could go on and on about what we went through and all the times we had to deal with professionals that knew her better than we did, even though we were living with her 24/7, but that would be another book or two.

I don't want to give you the wrong idea about Krystle. Most people who thought they knew her did not see this side of her. That was reserved mainly for me, Mike and the boys. Once in awhile she would slip up, mostly in school. There is another side to her. She is sweet, thoughtful and funny. I could not love her more if I had given birth to her.

I am proud of all the obstacles she has overcome and how she continues to work toward normalizing her life as much as possible. She amazes me with all that she has learned about her disability and to work with it the best that she can. In spite of the odds against her, she has been able to work at a job part-time and to go to college and maintain honor student status. All that energy she put into tormenting others is being put to good use now. She is a survivor! Makes you want to put that to some Reba Macintyre music doesn't it?

Jimmy Wayne Meets Meryl Streep?

I am a one woman man, except for "the one I've been dreaming of…" Actually, those are some of the words to the song "I Will" by Jimmy Wayne. Man, that guy can sing! His songs tell a story and as he says in one of his songs, "some people have been through hell" you can't help but know this is a guy who has had his fair share of troubles, but has worked hard to overcome them.

One of the songs he sings is "Kerosene Kid." It is about a kid who is treated differently by other kids because he is poor. The kid learns to keep his head up and be proud. He sings "One on One" about wanting time alone with his girl, *not me, unfortunately*. How many times when life gets to be too much do we wish we could have time alone with our significant other.

The song, "Where You're Going" *really* touches my heart. I think about the people I know and how hard they try to change their lives and leave the past behind them. Unfortunately, there are always people from the past that do their best to drag them down. Krystle is a good example of this. She made her fair share of mistakes as she struggled to become an adult, but eventually she decided she wanted more out of her life. She finished school, got a job and started college. Her former friends and biological family have tried to sabotage her, sometimes unknowingly. It can be heart-breaking to watch someone you love struggle to keep moving forward and to leave the past behind. The words "it's not where you've been, it's where you're going" truly is an inspiration for people like Krystle.

Another song Jimmy Wayne sings is titled, "Stay Gone." I have to admit I would like to see some of the people from Krystle's past, to stay gone.

Jimmy Wayne has a story to tell and a voice that can make a person stop and listen. I have never considered myself someone who would be "star struck" around celebrities. To me, they are just people like you and me. However, if I were to ever meet Jimmy Wayne, I'm thinking, I might not be too cool about it.

I have often been approached at stores, at work or on the street and asked, "do you know you look like Meryl Streep?" I wonder if that could be used to my advantage. *Would Jimmy Wayne want to meet Meryl Streep?*

The Church Family

The quaint little church on the hill is full, *maybe not always full,* of many people close to my heart. When Mike and I moved out of the Brookston area many years ago and eventually moved back, I told some of the people of this church, that they had really ruined it for us to go to another church. We could never find another church quite like this one and that is because you cannot replace family.

Like in any family, we had and still do have our "ups and downs." There is sadness due to the loss of some members, including my own father. We miss the pastors that leave but welcome the new ones.

Like any church we have struggles financially. Many people don't realize that even though it is a church, we still have to pay the usual bills. They do not mysteriously disappear. The electric, propane and phone companies do not hear our prayers. We have to rely on the money that comes in on Sunday morning as well as fund raisers. If those events are not supported, there is no money to pay these bills. Some people are under the assumption that grant money keeps the church going. I am not quite sure where they think these grants come from; who knows maybe they think God grants us money. That is not how it works, I'm afraid. We have to make our own way.

Through all the struggles the church endures there is always humor. We even laugh at funerals! I need to elaborate on that statement.

When my dad died, it was very sudden. He went to a council meeting the night before, though he wasn't feeling well. The next morning my mother called and said, "I'm taking dad to the emergency room." I offered to drive them, but mom said she would do it. They had to drive past our house and before they got that far, dad slumped over. Mom made it to our house. Mike called 911 and I ran out to the car to try to revive him. After an ambulance was called, Mike and I started CPR. I was not able to get a pulse. The volunteer fire department responded and was not able to revive him either. One of the most difficult things I ever had to do was to tell mom that he was gone and to call my sisters with the news. We were all devastated and in shock. Our church family was, as well.

We planned the funeral and our wonderful pastor visited us at my parent's house and listened to us reminisce about dad. That is not an easy task, given how difficult it is to draw us all out - actually it was just the opposite, we didn't shut up for a minute. The poor pastor was fiercely writing down notes, trying to keep up with us. He too, knew dad well from working together on the new addition of the church.

Pastor put on a memorable service. He had us laughing at some of the antics that involved dad. The whole service was amazing. My dad was very patriotic and as the coffin was carried from the church, the congregation sang dad's favorite song "The Battle Hymn of the Republic." What a wonderful way to celebrate dad's life!

As I sat by the Artichoke River, after my dad died, I contemplated his life. One thing that stood out in my mind was that through all the hard times in my life, dad's presence had a calming influence on me. He didn't have to say anything; he just had to be there. That made losing him that much harder, because this was one of the most unbearable experiences in my life.

You Were There

You were there when I was born
Your were there through milestones
You were there when I started school
You were there when I finished school

You were there, you were always there

You were there to walk me down the aisle
You were there to celebrate each new life
You were there through the happy times
You were there through the tragedies

You were there, you were always there

You are no longer there in my earthly life,
But you will always be there in my memories
You will always be there

I wrote this after my dad passed away.

The church "Women's Group," who meet once a month in the basement of the church, can never quite get through the meeting without going off on stories that do not relate to the business at hand. They can be heard laughing about all the things that happen at the events they organize. Every year they sponsor a Hunters Dinner (they don't do Hunter's Balls), a Christmas Cookie Sale along with a European Coffee/Tea House, a food stand on the 4th of July - just to name a few and most of the time the money is donated to a charity.

Everything is strictly done on a volunteer basis and is usually the same group of people doing the bulk of the work. These same people bring food and serve at funerals. It is a good thing they maintain their humor because THEY WORK HARD!

We are able to find humor in a lot of situations. My sister April said that she wanted to lose a little weight. Her incentive was a trip to the cities. Her husband Randy wanted to go to the cities before she finished losing the weight. She said, "I cannot go to the cities until I lose this weight."

We were sitting in the basement of the church discussing this, when one of the women who had a little weight to lose asked, "Why can't you go to the cities?" I thought I would help April out and explain. I said, "Well, you see they recently put in a weigh station before you get to the cities and April is over the weight limit so they won't let her through." This woman's response was "WELL I have a doctor appointment there next week AND I'M STILL GOING!" I don't recall telling her that I was kidding. Hopefully, she did not circle around the cities too much to avoid that nonexistent weigh station.

Now that I think about it, the funniest part about it is, April didn't have much weight to lose, so if she were over the weight limit, there would be an awful lot of people either stuck in the cities or not allowed enter.

Even the pastors are not infallible. Of course, we give them a hard time too. Here are just a few examples: a Pastor slipping on his shoe lace while bowling and falling into the gutter, another building a fire in the church fireplace on the end where the wood was stored and smoking the confirmation kids out of the building and more recently a Pastor who does not drink coffee, making coffee for the council members using the coffee scoop that was in the can for making coffee in the sixty cup coffee maker. He was making coffee in the twelve cup coffee maker. Made their hair stand on end! Can you just see the council members who are between the ages of forty and seventy sitting around the table with spiked hair and looking like they were high?

I could go on and on about this family too. Again, it would probably take another whole book.

Embarassing Moment

Mike and I were at my parent's house as well as some other family along with a person who used to be in the family - I'll call him "Shep" after one of my *favorite* childhood dogs. They're divorced now.

We were all hungry and decided to order burgers from a local bar. Shep said he would pick them up if I phoned in the order. He gave me the number to call. I dialed and a guy answered. I asked "is the kitchen still open?" He replied, "I'm not sure, what do you want?" I proceeded to order, "I'll need four hamburger baskets." He asked "with fries?" At this point I am thinking, *that's why they're called hamburger basket*s, but "yeah, that's what I want." He asked, "Anything else?" I ordered some pop to go with them and asked how long it would be before we could pick up the order. He replied, "Just a minute I have to ask "Betsy" if she wants to cook". That is when I realized, Shep gave me the wrong number and I had called the home of one of our church parishioners. Betsy's son had answered the phone and decided to play along.

The next morning was Sunday. That is when we go to Sunday morning worship. Betsy and her husband "Dan" were there. Every time Dan would look my way, he would start to laugh. I was pretty sure he was laughing *at* me. We went downstairs after the service for coffee. Dan finally could not contain his laughter any longer and of course he had to tell everyone what had happened. It still comes up occasionally even though it has been at least twenty years. It is always amazing to me how we cannot remember what we did yesterday, but we can remember something that happened twenty years ago, like it was yesterday.

The Ugly Vase

When my godmother, Hazel passed away, we were told to go to her house and pick out what we would like from her. My sisters and I didn't want to go. We didn't feel right about being there with her gone, going through her stuff. We were told that it was important to my great-aunt Alvina that we be there. Reluctantly, we did go. When we got there, some of the people were practically running from room to room grabbing up things. My sisters and I felt uncomfortable. Alvina saw we weren't taking anything and encouraged us to do so. April and I were standing there and Alvina picked up a gold plated vase that could have been a plant pot, I'm really not sure. She said, "Here, one of you take this." I told April "you go ahead." Neither one of us wanted it because it was just so ugly. Hazel's taste ran a bit on the gaudy side. Later, April tried to force it on me, but I won out. I put it in her van. April and her husband Randy came to our house to deliver some of our new possessions. After they left, I went to the basement, and there it was! - The ugly vase. THE WAR WAS ON!

I used it as an ice bucket with a bottle of beer in it and gave it to my parents on their wedding anniversary. They sent it to April and Randy from Wisconsin in a box that said "lollipop tree" on it. April was excited until she opened it. It showed up in my curio cabinet, thanks to April. I wrapped it up and left it in their motor home and when April found it, she thought Randy bought her an eagle figurine she had admired. Wrong again. Mike and I moved to Colorado, as we were unpacking, there it was again and April had written "welcome to Colorado" in paint. She figured that would end it. Not so!

I sent it back at Thanksgiving with a bunch of plastic orange and red turkeys in it along with anything else I could find. After I finished decorating it I showed it to my neighbor who liked doing crafts. I asked her what she thought. The look on her face was priceless. She was struggling to say something nice about it. I could only imagine what she was thinking, *Susan's usually so creative, and she must have a head injury.* I told her what was really going on and she said, "oh good, I couldn't think of anything good to say about it," which was music to my ears. I sent it to April.

We moved to Sandstone, Minnesota and there it was again. I held on to it for years, figuring I would let April forget about it. We moved back to Brookston and the vase came with us. I had it hidden in our closet. It had dents in it and all kinds of paint at this point. April saw it in there one day and at mine and Mike's 25th anniversary party, IT SHOWED UP AGAIN, PAINTED SILVER! She had our son Mitchell get it for her. The traitor!

I still have it and I have a plan. My plan is to cement it in their yard. I guess I better get to it soon! I sincerely, hope that will be the end of the ugly vase. My great aunt Alvina, who lived to be 102 years old, has no idea how much entertainment she provided for us that spanned over two decades and continues to do so. It probably won't end until one of us is in our grave and being older, I have visions of it lying to rest with me. I shudder to think of it.

Innuendos

Anyone reading this book may have already noticed that I have the tendency to say things that could be interpreted more than one way. (The Hunter's Balls) I am not the only one.

When Mike and I were getting ready to move into our first home, my sister Robin and my cousin Mary were helping me decorate. We were talking about what method we preferred when using screws and nails to hang pictures. The conversation went a little like this. Robin said "I like to pound it in." Mary said, "Not me, I like to screw it in." I said, "I like to pound it in part way and screw it in the rest of the way." WE WERE TALKING ABOUT NAILS AND SCREWS! We realized how it could sound to someone else walking in and burst into laughter.

April is the "queen of innuendos" and she is so innocent about it. We were at the bar; we really don't spend much time there, honest! It just sounds like we do. One of the local patrons was picking out songs on the juke box. He told April and Brenda to go ahead and pick the rest of the songs.

We had been kidding around with this guy, he had quite a sense of humor and he would come over to our table and tell us jokes. After awhile we started laughing before he even told the joke, knowing it was going to be funny. He would say "I can't tell this joke, you're already laughing." He would leave and come back to try again. He finally told us, we were a hard bunch of people to tell jokes to, because we thought *everything* was funny.

Getting back to the juke box, he told them to pick out songs that wouldn't make him cry. After April picked out a song, she went back to him and asked, in a very sarcastic tone I might add, "I picked out 'Little Willy," is *that* going to make you cry?" He looked crushed and replied "it might *now*." She really wasn't referring to any part of his anatomy, but the way she said it everyone had their doubts.

While we were living in Fountain Colorado, I met a woman who lived across the street from us. We became close friends and still are. Yasmine is German and grew up in Germany. They have a lot of German people there.

One day we were discussing a person who was very touchy and people would tread softly around her so as not to offend her. I told Yasmine "I am not going to pussy foot around her." Meaning that I would not censor everything I said to her. Imagine how difficult that would be for someone like me. Yasmine had this horrified look on her face and said "what do you mean?" I told her what I meant and she said "that is not what it means in Germany, my mother would wash my mouth out with soap if I said something like that!" In Germany, it is a nasty thing to say because it *does* refer to a part of a woman's anatomy. However, it did not take Yasmine long to use the expression, as well.

I love to use all kinds of expressions. I would often have to clarify what they meant to Yasmine, because in Germany they would mean something entirely different. Yasmine is very much Americanized now. She uses expressions I don't even know.

Homespun Hill

I have always wanted to be my own boss and to have a craft shop. I decided to take the plunge. Mike and I renovated part of the garage into a craft/gift shop. I decorated it in a country style with blue and yellow being the primary colors.

There was a round table with pastel chairs in blue, green, yellow and lavender in front of the window. Guests would sit at the table and have coffee and cookies in between shopping. *It was an awful lot of walking in those two aisles that were about six feet long.* There were shelves lined along three walls, curio cabinets with glassware, wall hangings and Christmas decorations, when they were in season.

I hung blue, yellow and green fabric on the high ceilings. The fabric was fashioned in a way that it resembled a quilt. My niece Emma stared up at the ceiling and said "Auntie Susan, you're the only person I know that hangs a quilt on her ceiling." Eventually, the fabric became stained and I replaced it. In the kitchen area, I hung vintage tablecloths on the ceiling. Of course, Auntie Susan is the only person Emma knows who hangs tablecloths on the ceiling too. *She really needs to get out more; where else would people put a tablecloth?*

I sewed table runners, quilts and many wall hangings. I wanted variety so I would paint wooden chairs, make tables out of clay pots and "shopped" in my cousin, Eva's barn and burning pile for items I could turn into masterpieces; *at least I liked to think so.* I stenciled on antique windows as well as furniture. Mike even got into the swing of things and would build me things to put in the shop.

HomeSpun Hill is no longer open. The chances of it surviving in a city of ninety eight people were not 98% let me tell you, but I had fun doing it for the three years it was open. The loyal customers that came to the shop will still come to craft sales when I have them. I donate the proceeds to whatever charity that strikes my fancy at the time.

Christmas

I LOVE CHRISTMAS! All year long I buy Christmas ornaments to mark a special time spent with family and friends during that year. When I decorate the tree, I become very nostalgic. I love reflecting back on the year and thinking about those special times. My favorite ornament that gets center stage on the tree is a little bedraggled angel that Santa left in my stocking one year when I was a child. *Not too terribly many years ago.* She has a plastic face, white angel hair that stands straight up, bendable arms and legs and wears a white lace dress with blue trim. She is only about three inches long. People laugh when I say, she is my favorite of all the ornaments, because I have some elegant looking ones, expensive ones and antique ones, but none come even close to her.

When our children were small, I loved to sit in the middle of the living room floor and wrap their gifts. I had to make sure they all worked, so I had a great time. Mike was working afternoons when I decided to get to work on the wrapping and I thought *a glass of wine would taste good about now.* We rarely had alcohol in the house, but we had bought a bottle of wine for Christmas. I opened it and poured myself a glass, went back to the living room and sipped on it as I wrapped gifts. It wasn't long before my glass was empty. I thought, *maybe I'll have one more glass, that tasted pretty good.* I refilled my glass. Before long that one was empty too and I thought, *I sure would like another glass of wine.* I went to the kitchen to pour another glass, as

I stood there I thought, *oh what the heck, I might as well take the whole bottle with me!*

When Mike came home, he took one look at me and my rosy cheeks sitting among all the hastily wrapped packages and said "you're drunk!" I replied, "No, I'm just wrapping Christmas gifts."

The next morning we went across the road to Dottie's house. Mike said to Dottie, "do you know what my wife was doing last night while I was working? She drank a whole bottle of wine while she was wrapping Christmas presents and she was drunk!" Dottie looked at me and said, "SUSAN why didn't you call me, I would have helped you!" It was the wine she wanted to help me with. That would have been a pretty picture for Mike to come home to. His wife and mother sitting on the floor among Christmas paper snokered!

One year I was at T.J. Max and spotted a hutch for putting miniature dishes on. I thought it would be cute sitting in my kitchen. I knew Mike wouldn't take the hint and I usually don't buy myself anything at Christmas time. I bought it anyway, wrapped it up and wrote on the tag, To: Susan From: Mike. I told the kids what I had done; they thought it was funny.

Christmas morning, Mike handed me the gift looking a little puzzled. He didn't remember wrapping that gift for me, he also didn't realize he could do such a good job wrapping, I'm sure. I un-wrapped the gift and exclaimed! "How did you know I really wanted one of these?" He looked confused and shrugged his shoulders. I asked him "where did you ever find this?" He looked a little flustered and said "I don't remember, but I knew you would like it." Nice try Mike! The kids and I all laughed and I told him the truth. He said "you think you're so funny." I did think so and so did the kids.

Another year, a friend of mine, Nancy gave me a Christmas gift. She noticed I had an antique chicken cage suspended from the ceiling over my kitchen table. I had chickens in there. Don't worry, they weren't real, I wouldn't want anything dropping into my morning coffee. She had found a chicken with feathers. I know most chickens have feathers unless they've been hen pecked but this one wasn't real or ceramic either. When I opened it, I couldn't help getting excited about adding it to the others. It was really pretty; it had orange, red and brown feathers. It looked a lot like a Banty Hen. I decided I would wait to put it up after Christmas. I carefully, put it back in its box and put it under the tree again. After Christmas, I went to get it, it was GONE! I looked everywhere. I had no choice but to tell Nancy that the chicken she gave me flew the coop. Now whenever I misplace something, I say, "I must have put it in a safe place with that chicken."

Christmas baking is a must in my house. It adds to the whole homey Christmas atmosphere. I try to make the kid's favorite cookies and I learned from a dear friend, Ellen who lived in Missouri, how to make Mike's favorite fruitcake. My mother also loved this fruitcake and *still does when I do it right.* Ellen did everything by memory and when she taught me how to make it, I had to write things down and guess at the amounts. I did really well with it too, except for the brandy. I recalled how she would soak the cloth in the brandy and then dump some more on the cake itself. We made it in the summer and froze it until Christmas.

After Ellen passed away, I started making the fruitcake on my own. The first year, I did everything just like she said, except I made it right after Thanksgiving so it wasn't in the freezer at all. I figured fresh must be better yet. I didn't know much about fruitcake. After the loaves were baked and cooled, I soaked the clean dishcloths in brandy. As I was dumping brandy on the loaves, I realized a pint wasn't going to be enough, so I sent Mike to buy more. I only used about half of that pint. I gave mom her fruitcake and the next day she told me, "next year you can make mine without brandy, because I was up all night, after eating that fruitcake!" My poor mother had a buzz going all night. I could just picture her zipping here and there all night long.

The next year I still added brandy but I used cheesecloth instead of thick dishcloths that really hold the brandy. I made it in the fall so it could be in the freezer for awhile. *Funny, I don't go through nearly as much brandy as I did before.* Now my fruitcake is sought after. There are still some people who wouldn't mind a lot of brandy on theirs.

It's funny how years ago women made delicious food from memory. My grandmother did the same thing, her specialty was baked beans. My mother had to learn to make them by watching Grandma do it and I had to do the same by watching my mother. Grandma always brought these beans on Christmas and every other holiday. They too were a tradition.

I love all the holidays, but Christmas is definitely my favorite, the Christmas Eve candlelight service, the décorating, the baking and just spending time with family and friends.

Heavenly Christmas

In 2003 my sister-in-law Patti suddenly died. She was only 45. One year later her aunt and my neighbor, whom I had known all my life also died. Both had cancer. After my neighbor died I sat by the Artichoke River and thought about the upcoming holidays and how difficult it would be for the families. Patti's husband John was still struggling with his grief. I decided to write some of these feelings down, but first I prayed to God to help me express the feelings I was having and my empathy toward the families. I sold several copies and the money was donated to the American Cancer Society. I have given copies to people who have suffered a loss at Christmas time as well.

HEAVENLY CHRISTMAS

Christmas in Heaven means:
I am at peace, I am loved.
I have contentment, I have no worries.

Christmas on Earth means:
I will be mourned, I will be missed.

My last gift to you is to let you know,
I am at peace this Heavenly Christmas!

Easter

Probably, a lot of people think spring when Easter rolls around. There are visions of tulips and daffodils, cute little bunnies running through the green grass. There's the pleasant scent of spring in the air and people dressed in their finest to attend church full of Easter lilies. It's quite a vision isn't it?

Let me tell you how it really is in Northern Minnesota. Rarely, do we have a warm spring. It has happened, but our typical Easter involves mud or snow. Luckily, it is warming up by then, it is no longer below zero. We wear our winter jackets to church and forget about those dresses!

This does not stop me from decorating outside for Easter. I love snow and I love to play in it. Instead of snowmen I will make snow Easter Bunnies. I make it as I would a snow man and add white cardboard ears, a nose with whiskers and buttons made out of colorful plastic eggs. I make a sign to put in front of it and write "HAPPY EASTER FROM MINNESOTA!" I take a picture and mail it to my southern friends and family.

When my children were younger, my mother would have an Easter egg hunt at her house. My sisters and I would bring our families and go hunting. My sister Robin was nine months pregnant one Easter. We had lots of snow. The egg hunt was still on. I helped with the egg hunt that year and I thought it would be great fun to watch a very pregnant Robin crawl through the snow. I tossed one of her plastic eggs across the snow bank.

She had to walk through deep snow to get to it. Pregnant ladies don't walk on snow, they sink! She did get her egg and finished the rest of the hunt as well. What we won't do for candy!

I don't want to misinform you; we have had some warm Easters. I remember one in particular. At the annual Easter Egg Hunt, my sister April, followed all her clues and tracked her basket in the trunk of an old car. One problem - the trunk wouldn't open. The back seat had to be taken out - like I said, "What we won't do for candy," - by the time April got her basket; her chocolate bunny looked like Frosty the Snowman after he got locked in the greenhouse. Unfortunately, there was no magic snow to bring her bunny back. She was sniveling about it, so she got another one after Easter.

The Easter Egg Hunts are a thing of the past, but what memories!

Slumber Party

My niece's, Emma and Elle are sisters and their birthdays are only a few weeks apart. Their mother, Gayle, told them they could have a sleep over and invite a few friends. I was there and told them I was coming to their slumber party. They're sleep overs not slumber parties, boy am I old! I told them I was wearing my pajamas and we were not playing video games. We would play "Pin the Tail on the Donkey," "Drop a Clothes Pin in a Bottle" and "Musical Chairs." I was sure they would say no way! They got excited and told me I could even ride the school bus with them. I asked, "Aren't you going to be embarrassed in front of your friends when I show up with pajamas and curlers in my hair?" No, they wanted me there.

The day of the party I put on pajamas, robe, slippers and big curlers in my hair. As I got in the car, I couldn't help thinking, *I sure hope I don't get pulled over or have a flat tire, I really don't want to explain this getup.* I made it without mishap. All the girls ran to the car to meet me and I discovered I really was the entertainment. Who needs clowns when you have Auntie Susan? We played the games and not once did anyone even hint at playing a video game. They had a great time and so did I.

God Has A Sense Of Humor

When we were living in Colorado, I would often pile the kids into our mini van at 3:00 in the morning and drive straight through to Minnesota. Actually, I didn't *pile* them in; I let them sit on the seats for comfort. It was a grueling drive, especially when there was no one to spell me off. I always left early so I could have all the daylight hours for driving. By the time I would get to Minnesota, it would be dark again.

About three hours into the trip, I hit a skunk. I didn't punch him, I ran over him, with my van. I needed to stop to use the restroom but I decided to wait until I got to the next town. I did not want to open the door and let the *divine* scent in. The next town was about an hour away, but I thought I could wait that long. I kept going and said a prayer asking for rain. God answered my prayer. It rained all the way to Brush, Colorado. Torture when you need to use the bathroom. It rained all the way through Nebraska, it rained in Iowa, it rained in Southern Minnesota and it rained ALL THE WAY TO BROOKSTON!

I learned a lesson that day. I already knew that God answers prayers. What I didn't know is to be specific in what you pray for because God has a sense of humor.

Oh yeah, and if you are wondering if I ever did stop for the restroom. Yes I did, there was no hint of skunk aroma, or rather stench, by the time I got to the next town. It would have made for a really, really long trip if I hadn't stopped, not to mention wet inside as well as outside.

Friendships

I have mentioned some of my friends already, Yasmine the German friend who grew up in, of all places, Germany. There is Nancy, the chicken friend. Here we go again, let me clarify that, she is not a chicken; she is a really normal human being, most of the time anyway.

Let me introduce you to Heather. Heather is a person who rarely lets life get her down. She is very much the optimist. One thing we have in common, we both like to change things in our houses.

We were discussing a room in her house and I mentioned if she didn't have a certain closet, the room would be bigger. She loved the idea and being one to "not let the grass grow under her feet," she got right on it. She stayed up all night and did the work herself.

She called me the next morning and said "Susan you are just going to laugh when I tell you what I did last night." She proceeded to tell me about working on the room, and then delivered the punch line. "I was using the hammer and it slipped and I broke my nose." I said, "THAT'S NOT FUNNY HEATHER!" She said "yes it is" and she was laughing. That had to hurt! I could take that as an insult - she must think I have a macabre sense of humor, but I know Heather and by the time she was through with her tale, it *was* funny.

I have a couple of friends from my high school days that I am still in touch with. One of them is also my cousin. Eva is probably most like me of all my friends except she is nicer, more talented and a lot prettier. Okay, so *maybe* we aren't as much alike as I thought. She home schools her children and does a fantastic job! She sings, plays the piano, great decorator and you know what? ENOUGH ABOUT HER! Let's just leave her on that pedestal and forget about her for awhile.

Kelly, I have known since I was in the twelfth grade. She is a year younger than me but looks older. I'm lying again, sorry. She and I don't panic in stressful situations; even when we were younger and I was driving down a one way street the wrong way. There were headlights in front of us and Kelly calmly said "I think we are going down the street the wrong way, there's a car coming at us." I responded "oh yeah, I think you're right" and calmly got out of the way of the oncoming car. We continued on like nothing out of the ordinary happened. Now, I ask you, aren't we the kind of people you would want to be in the car with?

I hate to say it, but that is not the only time I have gone down a one way street the wrong way, in my younger days. This story doesn't really fit in this section but I don't always do things the way they are supposed to be done.

I was on my way to visit my Grandmother who was in the hospital. If you have ever been to Duluth, you know all about the one way streets. There are a lot of them. I took one, the wrong way. I realized I was going the wrong way when I was the only one going down the hill and everyone else was coming up the hill, straight at me, including a police car. I have to admit when I saw him, I did panic this time. I hurriedly shifted into reverse and backed up around the corner, straight into a bread truck! To add insult to injury, there were two young guys standing on the corner pointing their fingers in my direction and laughing! HOW RUDE! Needless to say the police officer decided to have a chat with me. I explained I was on my way to visit my Grandmother in the hospital. He asked where I was from. I told him, "Brookston." What a break! He didn't know where that was and figured it was out in the boonies somewhere. This is one time I did not mind letting him think I was a "country hick" in the big city. He calmly explained about one way streets and sent me on my way. I was eighteen and not feeling very "groovy" at the time. *I grew up in the 70's.*

Sunshine

There is a special ray of sunshine in my life that I could not possibly avoid writing about. His name is Barrett. He is the son of my sister Gayle and her husband Brody. Gayle had some complications and actually had to have surgery while she was pregnant. I prayed everything would turn out for her and the baby. A feeling of peace came over me and I told Gayle, I knew the baby was going to be fine and he was. I was relieved she did not have to go through what I did when I lost "Baby Chris." *I often wonder if somewhere deep down I have made a connection between Barrett and "Baby Chris."* More likely, he brings back memories of Gayle when she was little; she was quite a character too.

To look in that boy's face is like seeing a ray of sunshine on a cloudy day. I know it sounds corny, but it is the best description that fits. However, one day he was throwing a bit of a temper tantrum and I told Gayle, "it's looking a bit cloudy today." I am sure he had good reason for his tantrum; his parents must have been picking on him.

He calls me, SuSu. Isn't that just the cutest thing you ever heard? He makes me feel special when he sees me. He has a big smile on his face and comes running with his arms outstretched. He can also break my heart. When Gayle tells him it is time to go home, he cries and screams and holds his arms out to me as she carries him out the door. *I just don't know what they do to that poor kid. It couldn't have anything to do with his being spoiled at Auntie SuSu's house, now could it?*

In August of 2008, Brody and Gayle had another bundle of joy. Grace Loreli was born and the clouds descended. Barrett was no longer the baby of the family. He loves his little sister but when Auntie SuSu holds her, not so much love then. As time goes on, he'll understand that he hasn't been replaced, there is plenty of love to go around.

I am thinking on Gayle's next birthday, I really should buy mom some flowers for keeping the baby. After all, if it weren't for Gayle, I wouldn't have my little ray of sunshine! Of course, Brody had something to do with it too.

I've Been Thinking

If there is ever a time that my boys wish they had picnic woods to run to, it would be when I say, "I've been thinking." When they hear those words, they know it means there in all likelihood, will be some heavy lifting involved. My husband pretends he doesn't mind, but judging from the dark cloud that passes over his face, he's perturbed.

I am known for changing things in my house a lot. I like to try different things and there is no better way to get rid of those dust bunnies than to move things around. There is another benefit and that is - it is *very* therapeutic.

I also paint the walls a lot. There are just so many cool colors; I have to try them all! The ones I like, that is. People often comment, that I am good at picking out colors and that they are afraid to try anything daring. I respond, "It is only paint, if you decide you don't like it, you just do it over." Some people look at me like they never thought of it that way before; others look at me and say; "Are you crazy? I hated painting it the first time around, why would I want to do it again?" The people who hate painting should probably stick with neutral colors and add color by way of pictures and other accessories.

I love antiques, so when I find something and buy it, I have to move things around to accommodate it. I do a lot of Goodwill shopping. I am not referring to shopping for someone else out of the kindness of my heart either. I buy *myself* stuff from the Goodwill. I have found some great deals on antique furniture. That is where the boys come in. I have been known to recruit nephews as well. One nephew asked me, "Why do you always have to buy such heavy furniture?" I replied, "Because I have strong sons and nephews to help me haul it." He looked at me and knew there was no use arguing, just go with the flow.

When we first moved into our current house, one of the first things I wanted to do was getting rid of the sliding glass door between the living room and the dining room. Of course, it only took about four years to accomplish this. When I first said "I've been thinking" and nothing got done about it, I wondered if maybe Mike did have his own picnic woods to run to. I probably don't want to know. One day, I decided to take action myself! My nephew Josh was visiting, who is another strong nephew - how lucky can one decorator be? I told him "I've been thinking," he didn't run so I pressed on. If you like demolishing things, you can take that door out for me. I didn't have to ask twice. Out came the crow bar and the door was history, with Mitchell's help.

Mike came home from work and said "you took the door out." The man's a mastermind, what can I say! He knew he had to frame in where the door used to be, but to his credit, there was not a cloud in sight. He got right on it.

I try to salvage what I can if something gets broken. This was the case of my gazebo that I had on the back deck overlooking the Artichoke River. Each corner had a decorative rod iron panel. One day we had horrendous winds and suddenly I saw my gazebo heading for the living room window! Luckily, it got hung up on the deck railing before it broke the window. The gazebo was ruined! Marshall and our nephew Matt took it apart and after looking at it for awhile and thinking about it for awhile - I know, just like dad - an idea struck! I'll make it into a window seat.

After I told Mike, "I've been thinking" and after the dark cloud passed, I asked him to cut a board for a bed we had in the garage. It was a wooden bed that came in two pieces with drawers in the bottom. With using only half of the bed it measured eighteen inches wide, perfect for sitting on comfortably. I took the corner pieces of the gazebo and put them on both ends of the window seat. Mike cut a board to fit across the top where plants could be put with the vines trained to climb down the rod iron panels. I was real clever when I thought to put it under a window. That is why I call it a window seat.

When I decorate and change things around in the house, I am usually very decisive, because I can always do it over again if I don't like it. There is one exception, however. The sunroom floor, which is now our living room, still does not have flooring. I ripped out the seventies carpeting. *We sooo had bad taste in the seventies.* I knew I did not want more carpeting. Hardwood floors were out because of the wood walls and ceiling. I didn't want to feel like I was living in a box. I brought samples of floor coverings home and still couldn't decide. Flooring isn't something you want to rip up just because you don't like it, unless it's seventies carpeting.

I decided to temporarily paint the floor. I used a dark red and dark green, not Christmas shades, I like Christmas but not in the middle of summer, and designed a tile-like floor. Some people actually thought they were tiles. I still haven't figured out what I want and it has been three years. "Living on Hansen time…living on Hansen time…" That would make a great song! Oops, it's been done by Don Williams - "Living on Tulsa Time".

Many guests will comment that they can visit one day and the next time it is completely different again. They exaggerate! *Well, maybe not.* The more stressed I am the more projects I come up with. Like I said - it's very therapeutic.

I do not limit my projects to just the inside of the house. I love to garden, rather I like to plant flowers and create flower beds. I HATE WEEDING. My sister-in-law Linda has told me weeding is therapeutic. I just don't see it. Decorating *is* therapeutic but weeding - that's just plain WORK!

Those strong men in my life come in handy outside too. Marshall is so used to my way of thinking, he will say "oh no, mom's thinking again." I know I better nab him on the spot before he has a chance to run. They have all had their share of hauling rocks, tilling and digging holes. Just so you know, I only ask for help when I absolutely cannot do the work myself - most of the time anyway.

The whole south side of my yard is full of pathways and gardens with arbors. There are lily gardens, weed gardens, hydrangea gardens, weed gardens, iris gardens, weed gardens and a memory garden with a metal arch over the entrance that reads, "Bless This Garden." Oh yeah, there are a few weeds too. Actually, I do weed, but once it gets too hot and humid, forget it, weeds just add greenery and interest to the garden.

"I've been thinking, I should add another counter in the kitchen, take a cupboard out and put the refrigerator there, move the dishwasher under the new counter. I'll need one of the guys to reroute the hose after I move the dishwasher. I'll need Mike to build the counter to my specification ...where is everyone anyway?"

Traveling

I enjoy traveling, but the trips I enjoy most are shorter trips. I have traveled with Mike, Mitchell, my mother, sisters and sisters-in-laws.

Traveling with my *blonde*, sister, April is an experience in itself. We went to the Little Fall's Craft Sale. Vendors come from all over the states. The craft sale is many blocks long and it takes more than a day to cover all the territory. It is about a two and a half hour drive from Brookston.

We got an early start and after we got there we shopped until April's trunk wouldn't close anymore. We had nothing to tie it down with, but she didn't care, she said "I'll drive fast enough and the wind will keep it down." She was kidding, I think. My Uncle Gordon who lived nearby wasn't taking any chances; he found something to tie it down with.

We were on our way home, when April thought she may have missed a turn. It was one of those rare occasions where we were talking so much, we weren't paying attention. I told her I wasn't sure either. She turned on the road we thought was the one to take us to Deer River. After going a few miles and getting farther into farm country, we were pretty sure it was a wrong turn. April was laughing and jokingly said "I think we'll go to Mille Lacs Lake, I always wanted to see it at night." I said "it sure would be nice to have a map about now." She agreed and approximately, twenty minutes later April said "there's a map in the glove compartment" - took awhile to process that in her brain I guess.

I took out the map and figured out where we were and started to laugh. "You're not going to believe this, but we really are headed to Mille Lacs Lake!" Because we were going the long way around, we needed gas. She was pulling into a station when I said, "you might not want to get gas here, because it costs over $3.00 a gallon." She looked at me like I was some kind of idiot and said "that's diesel!" She was right, I was an idiot. She pulled into the gas station and tried to get the nozzle to go into the gas tank, but it wouldn't go. Suddenly, a light bulb went off in her head and she laughed so hard she could hardly speak. She told me she picked up the wrong nozzle and was trying to put diesel in the car. Now who's the idiot? A two and a half hour drive took us closer to four and a half hours.

Randy and April's daughter Laura moved to Milwaukee, Wisconsin to attend Medical College. While we were moving Laura's furniture into her apartment, April drove into town to get pizza for everyone. When Laura and Asia asked their dad where mom was. He told them and they replied, "you let mom go alone in a strange city, AT NIGHT?" I told April how her daughters were concerned for her well-being. Funny thing, she took it as an insult.

Randy and April's other daughter Asia was attending college in North Dakota. She was very lonely, so I took my mother and went to visit her. We were sight seeing and I asked Asia for directions. She was still unfamiliar with the city and said "Susan, remember I am my mother's daughter." I told her, "Remember I am your mother's sister." I pointed at mom and said "she's your mother's mom. We *are* in trouble!"

I better clear something up here. April is a very intelligent person. She is a Department Manager at Wal-Mart and she is good at it. The store manager just had to give her a compass to navigate her way around the store, but hey once she finds her way back to her department she works hard! Okay, I just added that last part about the compass, but damn it's hard to say nice things about my sister.

If ever you want to take a fun-filled trip, I suggest you borrow my sister April. PLEASE!

My son Mitchell and I decided to take an impromptu trip. Mitchell had time off from work and we decided we would travel through Wisconsin and eventually make our way to Illinois. We saw *a lot* of Wisconsin! Nothing of Illinois! We kept changing our minds on what we wanted to do. We were within one hour of being in Illinois and we changed our minds again. Mitchell was in charge of the map and he would highlight our route. We would be driving south, and then decide to go west, then north, then south, then east, then south - get the picture? We never got lost though and we had a very colorful map of Wisconsin.

Thunk!

I was working overnights at a local boarding home for elderly and disabled people. After I got off work one morning, I went to Cloquet to get my hair cut. I checked in and went to sit down to wait.

As I walked to the six chairs in the waiting area, I decided to sit in the chair farthest away, near the wall. I remember walking toward that chair and thinking something just didn't feel right. After I walked straight into a floor length mirror, I realized what it was. Normally, when you are walking you don't see yourself coming toward yourself! It just didn't register! There were not six chairs, only three and I sat in the third one and was *sooooooooo* hoping no one saw me. That was not to be, however. I looked over to where my cousin was cutting someone's hair and saw her laughing. Bad enough to have someone you don't know see you do something stupid, *but family?*

Mike and I bought an older home to renovate. One of the things we planned to change was a sliding glass door between the dining room and the living room. We had not done that yet at this point, when we had a Thanksgiving gathering at our house. It wasn't the first gathering we had before it was changed. It took Mike, who was living on "Hansen Time," four years to get around to it and even then he didn't actually do it. Our nephew, Josh and son Mitchell took it out. I explain this because we have had Thanksgiving every year at our house so the door was no big surprise.

I was in the kitchen when suddenly I heard, THUNK! I went into the dining room and my son Michael was laughing; he walked straight into the closed door. A short time later, there was another THUNK! My sister Brenda walked straight into the door. She hung a sheet of paper on the door so no one else would have that problem. I don't think anyone else would have, but who knows? I felt pretty good about it myself because that had to have been one clean window! The alternative would be what were those two on?

I have to tell you the story about our white miniature poodle that we had when I was growing up. We treated him like he was one of the siblings. His name was Bimbo. We did not name him that because he was unintelligent or superficial, it was a name we had heard in a song, sung by Jim Reeves.

Bimbo, Bimbo, where ya gonna go-e-o
Bimbo, Bimbo, whatcha gonna do-e-o
Bimbo, Bimbo, does your mommy know
That you're goin' down the road to see a little girleo.

My sisters and I would dress him up and he thought he looked pretty darn good. He was struttin' his stuff; let me tell you - straight into the wall. He wasn't paying attention and we heard "THUNK!" Now that I think about it, Bimbo really was aptly named.

bim·bo [bímbō]
(plural bim·bos)
n (slang)
an offensive term for a man or woman who is regarded as being unintelligent or superficial

115

[Early 20th century. Origin uncertain: probably from Italian, "baby, small child."] Encarta ® World English Dictionary © & (P) 1998-2004 Microsoft Corporation.

Pet Stories

I grew up with a lot of pets and I would include Bimbo in this section but he was my brother and he deserves better than that.

Because I grew up with so many pets, it only stands to reason my children would too. In the time Mike and I have been married, we have adopted a lot of cats, dogs and farm animals. We like to pick special names for each one to reflect their unique personalities.

Sawed-Off was a Siamese cat with neurological problems. My sister Gayle's boyfriend at the time had given him to Mike as a Christmas present. Mike named him. How did that name come to be you ask? The boyfriend was short and Mike thought he was, oh so funny, when he would tease him and ask him how his legs got sawed off. Luckily, the boyfriend had a sense of humor.

Mitchell had a cat named Daisy and we had another named Lily. After Daisy had kittens we named them after flowers too, Rose and Iris. We were so clever and when we adopted an orange striped kitten we wanted to name him after a flower too. We thought and thought about it, Pansy - definitely not, Buttercup - done that, I know, how about Monkey Face? It was later I remembered the flower I was thinking of was, Monkey Flower. Monkey Face stuck. He was aptly named, he acts like a monkey; he climbs on everything! I took him to the veterinarian to have him neutered because I did not want anymore Monkey Faces. There was a woman with her dog there; I walked up to the receptionist and said "I am here with Monkey Face." No - Mike was not with me. Both the woman and receptionist started laughing; I did not know I was so funny.

We adopted a beautiful kitten from my sister Robin. He had long hair and was part Siamese. Any cat that gorgeous had to have a special name. I thought, Prince Charming? Sassy? He didn't seem to like those names so I figured I would think some more on it. In the meantime he was being very rambunctious and needed discipline. He was so cute that I would scold him and say, "You are such a little monster!" Guess what he decided his name was? He only answered to Monster.

Mike and I, along with our four children, were living on a farm in Sandstone, Minnesota. We thought it would be fun to have ducks, geese and chickens as well as our dogs and cats. My son's dog also brought home a baby pigeon and of course we raised it.

There was a chicken that escaped butchering from the previous owner and Mike found it and told me we had a rooster in the chicken coop. I thought that was great, especially when the rooster laid eggs. Mike didn't grow up on a farm.

My husband would go out to feed all of his "farm animals" and would call "AWESOME BABIES!" I have no idea why he called them that, but he did. They would all come running or flying toward him waiting for their food.

One day Mike and I decided to go for a walk. As we walked out the driveway, there were trees on either side of us. After we passed the trees there was a sharp turn to the right and fields on either side of us. This was one long driveway. We were just passed the sharp turn in the driveway, when I turned around and saw four geese, three ducks, two cats and a pigeon in a pear tree. Okay, okay I made that part up! There really were geese, ducks, cats and dogs following us, with the pigeon we raised, flying over Mike's head. I told Mike "I am not going to take a walk with all those animals following us; people will think we're the hillbillies of Sandstone." *Jeez!* That is not the impression I wanted to make on our new neighbors.

My nieces, Laura and Asia had goats that their parents wanted them to give up, because they *really* belonged on a farm. They talked us into it. THOSE GOATS WERE ON THE CAR, IN THE PUMPKIN PATCH, IN THE GARAGE, TAKING LAUNDRY OFF THE CLOTHES LINE - THEY WEREN'T FOLDING IT EITHER! I finally lost all patience and decided we needed to find a new home for them.

Mike knew a guy who lived on a farm that wanted our goats. Mike told them he could have them. They would have free run of the farm. Mike told me how excited the guy was and even mentioned he might consider breeding them. I told Mike, "He'll be waiting a long time, because they were fixed." Mike had no idea.

The longest living pet we had, was Lacey, she was seventeen years old when she died. Lacey was a black and white longish-haired dog. She was a German Shepard/ Dachshund mix. I know I know she was not the prettiest dog I ever laid eyes on but she was loveable. I don't want to think about how it was even possible for her to be conceived.

Lacey's head was the same size as her neck which made putting a collar on her difficult. The collar would slide right off. She had the long body and short legs of a Dachshund. She had the ears, tail, nose and head of a German Shepard. I would try to think of something funny to say about her, but I don't think I need to, if you can picture the way she looked.

We have a dog that is a rat terrier. She is white, brown and black. She thinks she is a cat. She jumps up on the table when she thinks we aren't looking, she purrs - though she doesn't sound quite the same as a cat and she imitates the cats when they are cleaning themselves. She sleeps in a cradle, curled up with Monkey Face. Niki loves to give hugs and has the gentlest looking eyes. Sounds like the perfect pet. There is another side.

One day Mike and I left to do some Christmas shopping. I had some Keebler Elf cookies on the table, still in the package. When we came home I noticed most of them were gone. I figured my sons had eaten them until I started finding cookies buried in laundry, among Christmas packages, between cushions and under pillows. I could be wrong, but I am guessing that Michael and Marshall didn't do that. Judging by the guilty look on Niki's face, I am pretty sure I know who did.

Tabitha is a Chocolate Lab/Springer Spaniel mix. She was born on the day my dad died. I sometimes wonder if she could be a reincarnation of dad. She gets this smirk on her face just like dad! Tabitha has a way of showing her teeth so it looks like she is growling but in actuality she is smiling. Dad didn't do that though.

All of our pets through the years have become actual members of our family. Mike and I are *proud* to say we have many grand-cats and grand-dogs - that is, until they come to visit.

Who Ran Into Whom?

People are always hitting deer with their vehicles along the country roads, highways and even in the city. There are a lot of deer. Once in awhile the deer run into people.

We were living in Sandstone when Mike and I came home from a shopping trip in Duluth. As we drove into the driveway we spooked a deer. Our son Marshall was walking across the yard and the deer took off and almost ran over Marshall. Marshall barely had enough time to jump out of the way. We couldn't help thinking that if the deer had run him over; it would be interesting, trying to explain to the hospital staff that a deer hit him instead of the opposite. I suppose we could have written a song, "Marshall Got Run Over by a Reindeer" - think it's been done already though.

Mike was working as a game warden and it was deer hunting season. He came home and said, "I got my deer today." I was puzzled by this because I thought he was working. He proceeded to explain, "The deer ran right into the side of my truck and put a dent in the passenger door." About three hours later, he came home again and said, "I got another deer, it ran into the other side of the truck and put a dent in the door." His boss told him, "Mike go home before you wreck the truck."

What are the chances of this happening twice in a matter of hours? The funny thing is we all tease Mike about how slow he drives. The way I figure it happened is, Mike was driving so slow that the deer was sure he would be long gone by the time he got to the side of the road, but BAM!

Mike was still passing by and the deer never knew what hit him or rather what he hit, as he was sure that truck was long gone by now.

Three hours later Mike was on another road and that deer probably thought - *I don't need to slow down, that truck will be long gone before I jump the ditch* - BAM! The last thought that deer must have had was - *there must have been another truck I didn't see.* But no, it was *still* Mike passing by.

Mitchell's Getting Married!

My youngest son sent me a text message to tell me about his girlfriend. He was shocked to learn that I figured out her name was Sam. I STILL KNOW EVERYTHING! Actually it wasn't too hard to figure out, as he talked about her often.

After a brief courtship, Mitchell told me he was going to ask Sam to marry him, but I had to keep it a secret. Eventually, he did ask her and she said yes. They told me the good news and also said I had to keep it a secret until they could tell Grandma themselves. TOO MANY SECRETS TO KEEP! Talk about torture! They finally told Grandma and I was telling everyone I could think of, the good news. I was a little excited. You may be able to tell by the Christmas letter I wrote.

Merry Christmas From The Artichoke River Smiths!

*I'll bet you are all wondering what that means! Well, let me tell you, **MITCHELL IS GETTING MARRIED!** I'll explain more as I go down the list of happenings in the Smith family.*

Michael is still working construction and has a boy named Jake that keeps sneaking up the road to see us. I feel sorry for him when he sits on the deck looking in, so I let him in and send him into the basement until Michael fetches him and chases him back down the road. We had a little scare, Michael said Jake threw up and heard a clunk in the kitchen, it turned out Jake had swallowed a little rock. He likes to carry rocks in his mouth. Oh yeah, did I forget to mention Jake is Michael's dog.

Mitchell is getting married in March. I'll tell you more about that later.

Marshall is still a security guard at the Black Bear Casino. He lives at the bottom of the hill with Michael and their pets. They do have shelter. He still helps us around the house a lot. He still likes to fix things that are broken and maybe not so broken until he fixes them. It's great to have him nearby, I can always count on him to help me out when I come up with ideas, which I occasionally do. He will often ask me what I am doing and when I say, "I've been thinking" he will always say "mom's thinking again!" I just know, he means that in the best way possible, because he always helps me with the heavy work.

Mitchell is getting married to a girl named Samantha, more about that later.

Krystle is living in Duluth and working at Starbucks. She loves her job and is quite good at it. She recently told me, she is learning things about coffee and tea she never knew. I was so proud. I was able to teach her something too. She said she has a hard time sleeping sometimes. It turns out she enjoys the coffee at Starbucks too. I suggested she switch to a little decaf later in the day. She did and says it has made quite a difference. I can only imagine Krystle on a lot of caffeine; I did not have "visions of sugarplums dancing in my head." I had visions of Krystle with her legs wrapped around her head as she used to do when she was little, while watching T.V. She was very limber.

Mike is a Game Warden and I still do what I do but let's get on with what Mitchell is doing.

*We are a <u>little</u> excited about this next bit of news, though we hide it well. **MITCHELL IS GETTING MARRIED!** He and Samantha are getting married on*

March 8, 2008. Sam and Mitch met at Wal-Mart where they both work. They found a house in Brookston along the Stony Brook. Recently, a cousin mentioned she had visited the Smith's. I was a little taken aback at first until I realized she was talking about Mitchell and Sam. You probably already know where I am going with this, if not figure it out because I want to tell you about Mitchell and Sam. **THEY ARE GETTING MARRIED!**

Merry Christmas and Happy New Year!
Love Mike and Susan

P.S. One last thing, **HOPE TO SEE YOU AT THE WEDDING OF MITCHELL AND SAM!** *(The Stony Brook Smiths)*

The wedding plans had a few glitches. One bridesmaid had to be replaced, some of the guests didn't get their invitations, my aunt and uncle got theirs - only problem with that was, it was my uncle's name on it with a different aunt's name. A little wife swapping among family?

Sam's grandfather died suddenly the week that Sam's mother took vacation to sew all the bridesmaid's dresses, as well as her own. She was STRESSED! If that weren't enough the poor woman came down with bronchitis.

The engagement picture in the *Duluth News Tribune* had wrong information, *I cannot imagine how that happened and I am pretty sure Sam's mother can't either,* as well as the church newsletter that was sent out to the community with the news of the upcoming wedding of Michael Smith to Samantha Robison. The following month I wrote the following correction:

"Some of you may have been surprised when you read in last month's newsletter that my son, Michael, is getting married on March 8 to Samantha Robison. You were no more surprised than Samantha and Michael, not to mention my son, Mitchell, who really is marrying Samantha in March."

We, of course, had a good laugh over that one and we all know it is really Mike's and my fault, for naming our boys - Michael, Marshall and Mitchell. What can I say, we thought we were clever, but we were young.

I told Sam, "We are getting all the glitches out of the way before the wedding and on the day of the wedding everything will go off without a hitch." She replied, "There will be one hitch, Mitch and I are getting hitched!"

The Wedding

The weather on the day of the wedding turned out to be a really nice day for being March in Minnesota. We didn't have to have anyone on stand-by to pull guests out of the snow banks with their four wheel drive trucks.

Everyone ran around getting last minute things done and at 3:00 in the afternoon, one of the most momentous occasions in the Smith's and Robison's lives began. Our children were about to unite as a married couple.

It was a beautiful ceremony. The groom wore a black tuxedo with a blue vest and the groomsmen wore black with lavender vests. Each groomsman escorted the bridesmaids up the aisle. The bridesmaids looked beautiful in their gorgeous lavender gowns that were made by the bride's mother. Suddenly, there was the sound of rushing little feet coming up the aisle. The ring bearer dressed in his little tuxedo was on his way…let's get this show on the road! One woman made the comment that she had never seen a ring bearer move so fast. *He was pretty speedy.*

Things slowed down a bit after that. The ushers rolled the white carpet down the aisle. The flower girl in her little white dress walked up the aisle dropping lavender flower petals on the carpet. She did it to perfection.

The big moment came when everyone stood to see a radiant Samantha escorted by her father up the aisle. A beautiful bride she made. She was dressed in a white flowing strapless gown with black etched flowers and vines down the front and back. The love on Mitchell's face for

Samantha was hard to miss as she walked up the aisle. They really are a wonderful couple.

The pastor who performed the ceremony, not only gave a great sermon, he sang "The Lord's Prayer" and there were a few tears. A lot of those tears came from the bride's mother. Okay, I lied. It was Mike. *Maybe, it* was me. Later, I found out Sam and Mitchell had bet whose mother would cry first. Mitchell won. However, Sam's mother admitted she was close until she looked over at me and saw how much I was crying. She thought she would make me laugh by sticking her tongue out at me, unfortunately, I didn't see it, but the photographer caught it on camera. What a lovely picture of the bride's mother and there I sat oblivious to the whole thing.

Following the wedding ceremony, the guests moved on to the reception hall. The wedding party remained at the church for pictures and then, they too went to the reception hall. It seemed like a good idea for the wedding party to show up too.

The food was great! There were meatballs, chicken and ham, salads and fruit cut to perfection. The caterer was someone the couple had worked with and really went all out to make their reception memorable. To have that kind of food at a reception would have cost an "arm and a leg," but lucky for us, we were able to keep our body parts, because we paid mainly for the food itself and the caterer's helpers.

Mitchell's Aunt Terri made the two-tier cake. It had lavender silk flowers on white butter crème frosting. At the top of the cake - you guessed it - sat a bride and groom cake topper. The cake was one of the most beautiful wedding cakes I have seen in a long time. It was easy to see, that a loving aunt had made the cake for a special nephew and his new wife. It was a work of art!

The hall was decorated with lavender, purple and blue. On the table next to the cake sat a long mirror with blue lace along the edges. Each corner of the mirror had blue hydrangeas glued to them. On the mirror itself, were glass candlesticks with lavender taper candles and a white bowl between them with doves sitting on the rim. *The doves were not real, it would have been a mess, I am pretty sure there would have been something besides candles floating in the water otherwise.* Inside the bowl were blue glass stones, lavender rocks and purple-rose shaped candles floating in the water. Above the mirror, was a Precious Moments wall hanging, I had sewn, with Sam and Mitchell's names printed on it, along with the date of their wedding. There were purple tablecloths *on the tables of all places; they wouldn't let me put them on the ceiling,* with miniature champagne glasses and candles for centerpieces. The wedding party's table had the same centerpieces along with two large crystal candle holders that had crosses etched on them.

Following the reception, there was a dance with music by a D.J. There was no booze allowed, *of course, a few managed to find something in their vehicles to drink - imagine their surprise when they hit the jackpot, I am sure they had no idea how the booze got into their vehicles* and the ones who did find something to drink did not over-indulge.

Often at dances it takes awhile for the guests to warm up to dancing, it usually takes a few drinks - not at this dance, people got up right away and they were sober! The children who were anywhere from age two through twelve, danced right away and **they were sober too!** There was the usual dollar dance, the bride threw her bouquet and the groom threw the garter. They were caught by children and I'm thinking *it is going to be a looooong time between weddings.*

I could not have been prouder that day, if not a little sad too. My baby boy was moving on to a whole new life and so was our son Michael.

Michael Drops A Bomb

The title of this section could be misleading. Michael didn't pass gas. If he had it may not have taken us by surprise since that would not be anything out of the ordinary. (Kidding of course) He also did not blow up anything, except maybe his mother's sanity.

I was working on centerpieces for the upcoming wedding at the dining room table - in the dining room where we keep the table - when my son Michael walked through the front door, he opened it first, remember, this is the son who walked into the sliding glass door on Thanksgiving. He asked, "Mom do you know where my birth certificate and high school diploma are?" I told him where they were. I thought to myself, *he must be thinking about going back to school.* WRONG! He said, "I joined the National Guard today." "What?" I said. I had actually heard him but I was hoping I heard him wrong. He repeated it and I have no idea what I said after that or if I said anything at all.

He visited Grandma and told her. She was surprised, but told him that she was proud of him. Next, he told his uncle John. John shook his head and didn't have anything to say. John had served toward the end of the Vietnam War, but was in Germany. He no doubt was thinking about his own experiences. I told his dad, Mike when he came home from work and he too had been in the army. I said, "Michael joined the Guards today." Mike replied, "Why?" I told him, "He wanted to." End of discussion for the time being.

The next day, I told Michael that we supported his decision. He told me that his uncle John didn't seem to want to talk about his joining the Guard. I explained to him "it isn't like you led up to it. You just dropped a bomb on us and no one knew you were even thinking along those lines. It takes time to process that information." Of course, I didn't tell him, I did the same thing to his dad.

Michael is a weekend warrior, unfortunately because we are still at war that could change. We worry, but we are proud too!

March 5, 2008

Today, I had a feeling of dread. Michael went to the cities to sign the paperwork for the guards. He came home and said "I'm going to be gone for a long time." I asked him how long and he said, "three years to start with." I asked him if that meant he joined full time. He said no, "I'll be gone for three years and then I'll be back and only have to go on weekends." I told him that meant he was full time. Apparently, he didn't think I would be able to figure that out; he was trying lead up to it, but hadn't expected me to be smart enough to figure it out. So I went upstairs and I cried even though I knew he had made the right decision for him and I would support it.

Wedding Guidelines

Over the years, I have had the privilege to help plan or to be a part of weddings for important people in my life. The first wedding I helped plan was my own and the last being my son's. In between there have been sisters and friends.

Every wedding is unique, because there are no two couples alike and every wedding has its glitches. Most of the time the guests don't know about them and other times they may just add humor to the wedding. One thing they all have in common, they have their stressful times. If ever the wedding couple or the parents are going to go insane, this would be the time. That would certainly make for a memorable wedding - the couple and their parents walking up the aisle looking like escaped patients from a mental institution and I'm thinking most couples don't want that particular memory attached to their wedding.

There are many types of weddings. There are large, small, formal, casual, church or outdoor weddings. Some take months to plan and some may only take hours to plan.

My sister Gayle chose a small wedding. She called me on December 30th and asked if I would help coordinate her wedding. They wanted to get married on New Year's Day. She was not talking, a year away either! We had less than two days to pull it all together.

Gayle had to have unexpected surgery. Brody's place of employment would not let him have the time off because they weren't married. They were already engaged so they decided to get married sooner.

We had one whole day to get her dress, rings, food for the reception, the service planned and the bouquets made. Luckily, the church was still decorated for Christmas, so we just added white tulle to the red ribbons and made an archway between the rows of pews for her to walk under.

The pictures of the wedding were absolutely beautiful. There was less stress because of expectations not being so high. The guests did not mind getting phone calls instead of invitations - given the situation. Most people made it to the wedding too.

Gayle has never been a very decisive person, but one thing I said to her was "you are going to have to make quick decisions, if we are going to pull this off." She did a fantastic job; she and I even had time to celebrate New Year's Eve!

The reason this wedding came together so well was because everyone involved worked together and determined who would do what. Mom and Gayle did all of the phone calls to invite people. Mom and I gave our opinion on a wedding dress and Gayle made a final decision. Brody and Gayle took care of rings, marriage license, etc. In other words, everyone had a job to do and did it. It also helped that it was a small intimate wedding.

No matter the type of wedding, the roles all need to be defined. Who is going to be in charge of what and this needs to be determined by the parents and the couple. Traditionally, the bride's parents would coordinate this, but it is not set in stone. Throw out some of those old traditions and determine what works for your own situation. Remember, every family and situation is unique. In Sam and Mitchell's situation, the bride's grandfather passed away unexpectedly. This placed added stress on her parents and you can imagine the emotions they were experiencing. If they would have had to do everything, imagine the whole "mental institution scenario."

The most important people to keep in mind when planning a wedding, is the couple because it is their wedding. They should make all the final decisions and everyone else needs to respect that. Everyone involved in the wedding should do their best to make the day a special one for the couple because after all, this is one of the most important days of their lives and the focus should remain on them.

If you are asked to participate in any aspect of a wedding, treat it as an honor and not like you are doing the couple a big favor.

It doesn't matter what type of wedding, decisions have to be made and it is important to stick to it. After a decision has been made, move on to the next order of business. If the people planning the wedding are unable to do this, it could lead to a lot of unnecessary expense.

The day before the wedding, everything possible should be done. Bring everything to the place where the wedding and reception will take place. The less there is to do on the day of the wedding, the less stress there will be.

The siblings should offer their support. Offer to help and if the couple or parents want the help, ask specifically what they would like you to do and stick to that task and let everyone else do theirs. Most importantly, <u>do not join the army, a cult or gang the week of the wedding, it freaks the parents out and they are already stressed.</u> *You may want to rethink the cult and gang even after the wedding.*

The caterers need to have a list of what they do and what the family is responsible for. Do they make punch or *not*, coffee? Have the caterer make a list of food that is agreed upon. Whoever is in charge of the food, find out how much experience the caterer's helpers have had, as well as the caterer.

The wedding party should help to make sure things go smoothly. It is an honor to be asked to participate, treat it as such. This is an important occasion in the couple's life. *This day is not about you, it is about them.*

The guests, believe it or not have a responsibility as well. Again, keep in mind this is an important day to the couple and their parents. You have been chosen to celebrate with them. Do not sit around the table criticizing the event, if you must do this, save it for later. Do not tell the couple and their parents how they could do things differently, it's too late and I am pretty sure they *do not* want to do it over to meet everyone else's expectations. Besides, in all likelihood, the parents will not be available because they are now vacationing in that aforementioned facility. There is no such thing as a perfect wedding, except for Mitchell and Sam's of course, so keep in mind that when the big day arrives try not to stress the small stuff; it is too late to make changes now and really the important part of the day is seeing the couple united.

Building Screwed Up Memories

Now that I have a daughter-in-law, it is my turn to build memories. I have talked about memories of my mother-in-law; how we laughed over the Mounds Bars.

One day Sam called and asked if I would supervise her making Mitchell a robe for his birthday. We thought it would make great bonding time. Sam had already laid out the material with the pattern pieces on it and had done it perfectly. I told her we needed the front pieces to sew the pockets on.

As Sam sewed, I reminisced about my in-laws. I told her the story about how my sister-in-law Joan was sewing pajama bottoms for my boys. Dottie had given her the pattern and material. Dottie had already cut them out and they were ready to be sewn. As Joan sewed them, she thought to herself - *"these seem awfully big for someone so small."* After they were sewn she realized she could probably put two kids in them. She called her mother and told her the dilemma. Dottie asked her if she sewed both pairs, apparently Joan thought there was only one pair, no wonder two kids would fit into those pajama bottoms, she had sewn them all together. Sam thought that was a funny story.

After the pockets were sewn on the front of the robe, things just weren't matching up very well. I commented that I did not understand why the front of the robe was so much shorter than the back. We puzzled over this for awhile and suddenly, Sam realized she had grabbed the front sleeve and not the front of the robe. She had sewn the pocket on the sleeve! We had a good laugh and after ripping out the pockets, I told her "from now on it should be much easier."

I pinned the front shoulders to the back and she sewed it. I went home and she called awhile later and said "mom guess what happened when you pinned the shoulders together?" I guessed I had put the right side against the wrong side, instead of right sides together. That is exactly what happened. Out came the seam ripper again and so the Smith tradition of building screwed up memories, lives on. *By the way, the robe turned out great; it just took a little longer getting there.*

Graduation Ceremony

Over the years, I have been to many graduations; however I have never had the honor of attending an army graduation. My son Michael's was the first for me and the experience will forever be etched in my mind.

The graduation started with the "Charlie Company's" drill sergeants marching to the beat of a cadence on stage. The whole auditorium came alive with the shouts from the sergeants and the answering soldiers. As the soldiers took their places on one side of the auditorium, the National Anthem was sung.

After everyone in the audience took their seats, men and women who had served their country were asked to stand as tribute was paid to them. As I looked around at former soldiers they still had the proud stance of an American Soldier as the audience clapped. It didn't matter how many years had passed, the patriotism was still inbred. I couldn't help thinking of how proud my own father would have been, having served in the Korean War.

As the room quieted down again, the lights were dimmed on the stage. There was a round light on a dark background and a soldier in combat uniform entered onto the stage. He kneeled down on one knee, resting the butt of his rifle on the floor and all that was visible was the soldier in shadow. *THE SOLDIERS CREED* was read:

I am an American Soldier.

I am a Warrior and a member of a team.
I serve the people of the United States and live the Army Values.
I will always place the mission first.
I will never accept defeat.
I will never quit.
I will never leave a fallen comrade.

I am disciplined, physically and mentally tough, trained and
proficient in my Warrior tasks and drills.

I always maintain my arms, my equipment and myself.

I am an expert and I am a professional.

I stand ready to deploy engage, and destroy the enemies of
the United States of America in close combat.

I am a guardian of freedom and the American way of life.

I am an American Soldier.

There were speakers, a video of the training the soldiers had received over the past weeks and awards were given.

The big moment came when the pinning of the Engineer Branch Insignia was performed. Each individual soldier ran up on stage and shouted his/her name and what state he/she was from.

The Engineer Regimental Song was performed followed by *The Army Song* as the soldiers marched out of the auditorium.

The whole auditorium was alive with patriotism. Everyone there could not help but feel proud of not only their soldier but to be an American. It is an experience that will forever be etched in my heart and soul.

THE ENGINEER REGIMENTAL SONG

Pin the Castle on my collar,
I've done my training for the team.

You can call me an Engineer Soldier,
The Warrior Spirit has been my dream.

Essayons, whether in war or peace,
We will bear our red and our white.

Essayons, we serve America,
And the U.S. Army Corps of Engineers.

Essayons! Essayons!

THE ARMY SONG

First to fight for the right
And to build the Nation's might,
And the Army goes rolling along.

Proud of all we have done
Fighting till the battle's won,
And the Army goes rolling along.

Then it's Hi! Hi! Hey!
The Army's on its way,
Count off the cadence loud and strong.

For where're we go,
You will always know,
That the Army goes rolling along.

On December 12, 2008, Michael will be deployed to Iraq for up to eighteen months.

To Agree Or Not To Agree

Each story that I have shared in this book is the absolute truth, with maybe a few exaggerations, which I guess does not make it absolute. I don't know if my family and friends recall each story exactly the same way that I do, but I have written each story "THE WAY I REMEMBER IT."

Recipes

SuEllen's Fruit Cake

This is Ellen's recipe with a few of my own additions to it.
Hence the SuEllen.

1 Cup White Sugar
1 Cup Oleo or ½ C. Butter & ½ C. Shortening
1 Cup Dark Corn Syrup
½ Cup Coffee
(Brewed, don't make the mistake I made with the Instant
Potatoes in the Mounds Bars)
Mix with ½ Cup Orange Juice with Cooled Coffee
Cream above ingredients and add 4 Eggs, one at a time

In separate bowl from creamed mixture:
1 Teaspoon Salt
2 Teaspoons Nutmeg
¾ Teaspoon Cloves
2 Teaspoons Cinnamon
Add to approximately 2 cups Flour

Add to creamed mixture. Add more Flour if needed to get
"cake like" consistency

In separate bowl mix following fruit together:
Mixed Fruit with little or no Citron
Dates, Raisins, Green & Red Glazed Cherries, Glazed
Pineapple, Diced Apricots, Flavored Craisins - Optional

Add Walnuts and Pecans to Fruit

Add Fruit mixture to batter

Put in greased and floured bread pans –
either 2 large or 3 small pans

Bake at 300 degree oven, approximately 1 hour –
Cool in pans

Wrap in Brandy soaked cheesecloth and wrap in plastic or
Ziploc Bags

Freeze until ready to eat

*** Caution - go easy on the Brandy if you don't want to be
up all night! ***

Grandma Reed's Baked Beans

1 large bag of Great Northern Beans
Soak beans in large kettle overnight

Next morning add ¾ teaspoon Baking Soda
Boil for a few minutes
(My understanding of this, is to prevent people from getting
"gas" from eating too many beans, you be the judge)

Rinse beans and put clean water on

Add:
1 Onion
Salt Pork
¼ C. Molasses
¼ C. Ketchup
1 C. White Sugar
Salt & Pepper

Bake in 350 degree oven
When almost done, add 1 tablespoon vinegar

You'll just have to guess when you think they are done, that is what I have to do, because Grandma did not have a recipe to go according to.

Enjoy these family favorites, but go easy on the Brandy and don't forget to boil the beans in Baking Soda!

Mounds Bars

Ingredients:

Instant Potatoes - <u>PREPARED</u>! 2 servings
1 lb. Powdered Sugar
1-14 oz. Bag Coconut
1 t. vanilla
Pinch of Salt

Directions:

Combine all ingredients until well mixed. MAKE SURE THE INSTANT POTATOES ARE COOKED! (It helps to have moisture in order to roll into balls) Place in refrigerator until very cold. Form chilled mixture into small mounds. Place on cookie sheet. Refrigerate again. In a double boiler, melt 1-12 oz pkg. chocolate chips with ½ bar of wax. Cover each mound with melted chocolate.

Now days, I prefer to use Almond Bark.

More recipes on the following pages, taken from a cookbook I made for my children for Christmas, 2008. "Smith Family Favorites"

That Noodle Stuff!
Favorite of: Mitchell

1 Jar of Ragu Alfredo Sauce
1 Package Egg Noodles Cooked
Parmesan Cheese

Drain Noodles, add Alfredo Sauce
Mix and Heat
Add Cheese to Taste

* If you want a better recipe, ask Sam, she makes it better.

*** Mitchell always loved this hot dish and never had a complaint, until he got married and informed me, "Sam makes it better." I'll bet mine is easier to make, though.

Mom's Spaghetti
Favorite of: Mitchell & Krystle

1# Hamburger - Cooked
1 Large Can Tomato Sauce
1 Jar Spaghetti Sauce
1 Small Can Tomato Paste
Spices: Basil, Garlic Powder, Onion Salt, Oregano to Taste
A Little Bit of Sugar

Put in Crock Pot and Simmer all Day
Cook noodles, Pour Sauce over Noodles when done.
Top with Romano or Parmesan Cheese if Desired.

* Or have Michael make it, his is better!

*** Mitchell strikes again! Mitchell always thought I made the best spaghetti until he visited Michael in Hinckley, MN. He told Michael "this is the best spaghetti I ever had!" Of course, Michael couldn't wait to share that information with me. Mitchell still thinks mine is the best, he just wanted to make his brother feel good, I think.

Peanut Butter & Jelly
Favorite of: Mike (Dad)

2 Slices of Bread, Wheat or White
A Dollop of Jam or Jelly, any Flavor
A Spoonful of Peanut Butter

Take one Slice of Bread; smear Peanut Butter in the Center, ripping the Bread slightly.

Drop Jelly in Center, use other slice of Bread and Squish Together.

Take big bites, if you want to Taste the Peanut Butter & Jelly!

* Don't let Mike/Dad make it if you want P.B. & Jelly spread across the entire slice of Bread.

*** To this day, the kids will talk about how their dad would make them peanut butter and jelly sandwiches and plop everything right in the middle of the bread and squish them together. Of course, when they describe how he puts the two slices of bread together, they tend to exaggerate. *I don't know where they get that from!*

Krystle's Specialty
Not so Favorite of: Dad

2 Slices of Stale Bread
A Dollop of Jelly

Place Dollop of Jelly between the two slices of Bread &
smash together. Throw in Lunch Box & Top it off with a
Rotten Apple & a Can of Pop.

*** When we were living in Fountain, CO, five year old Krystle decided to pack a lunch for her dad to take with him to work. He discovered what he had in his lunchbox only after he sat down to eat during his lunch break. SURPRISE!

Pineapple Bread Pudding
Favorite of: Mitch, Sam, Krystle & Marshall

½ Cup Butter, softened
1 Cup Sugar
½ teaspoon ground Cinnamon
4 Eggs
1 Large can of Crushed Pineapple
6-8 Slices of Bread, cubed
¼ Cup Chopped Pecans, unless Sam is eating it, then <u>OMIT</u>

Preheat Oven to 325 Degrees. Beat butter, sugar & cinnamon about 1 minute. Add eggs; beat on high speed until fluffy. Fold in pineapple, bread & pecans. Pour into buttered dish. Bake until knife comes out clean.

Serve with caramel topping & whipped cream.

*** I found out after I printed the cookbook, Krystle never really like it. I guess you never really know your own kids!

Macaroni & Cheese
Favorite of: Marshall

Go to Grocery Store and buy a box of the cheapest Macaroni & Cheese you can find.

Take home, put kettle of water on to boil, forget about it for awhile, go watch T.V. and come back and add more water because it boiled down.

Follow instructions on the back of box.

* Have dad make it, if you want meat in it. Buy a package of hot dogs, he'll slice and add to Mac & Cheese. Ummmmmmmmm!